ALLEN CLARKE'S ADVENTURES IN INVESTING

Allen Clarke's

ADVENTURES IN INVESTING

How to Create Wealth and Keep It

KEY PORTER BOOKS

Canadian Cataloguing in Publication Data

Clarke, Allen B. (Allen Bradley), 1945-
Allen Clarke's adventures in investing: how to create wealth and keep it

ISBN 1-55263-281-4

1. Stocks. 2. Investments. 3. Finance, Personal. I. Title.

HG4521.C475 2000 336.63'22 C00-931704-X

Le Conseil des Arts du Canada depuis 1957 | The Canada Council for the Arts since 1957

The publisher gratefully acknowledges the support of the Canada Council for the Arts and the Ontario Arts Council for its publishing program.

We acknowledge the financial support of the Government of Canada through the Book Publishing Industry Development Program (BPIDP) for our publishing activities.

Key Porter Books Limited
70 The Esplanade
Toronto, Ontario
Canada M5E 1R2

www.keyporter.com

Design: Amy Seagram

Printed and bound in Canada

00 01 02 03 04 6 5 4 3 2 1

Dedication

To my father and mother, for placing such a high value on education and hard work in our family. My parents ran a corner store and one afternoon while I was working there my father noticed me put a small item a customer had bought into a bag. “Don’t use a bag unless the customer asks for one,” he explained. “We have to pay for those bags.” So, for teaching me overhead cash-flow burn rate and EBITDA before I could even drive, and always being there, even now, thanks.

Acknowledgments

First things first: thanks go out to Miss Baker, my grade 5 English teacher with whom I spent two of the best years of my youth, and to Dr. W. C. Ferguson, my high school English teacher, who somehow made Shakespeare interesting to a bunch of teenage boys. Without some appreciation of English and the written word, this book would not be possible.

Of course, there are the usual suspects to thank—my wife, who was the catalyst for my leaving Kingston and entry into the financial industry, and my daughter, who after studying English at Oxford this summer compiled the index for this book in a fraction of the time it would have taken anyone else.

To John Smith and Glen Moore, who took Clarkeeee under their wings when I started in the brokerage business at McLeod Young and Weir—it made all the difference, thanks.

Special mention and thanks must go to Jim Carr—if he hadn't grossly misrepresented how much work it is to throw together a meaningful book on investing, I never would have begun, and also for remaining a steadfast supporter of the project to the end.

And finally heartfelt gratitude to Joe McDonald, whose support and vision at just the right moment made both Opus 2 Direct and this book come to life.

"And you to whom adversity has dealt the final blow / With smiling bastards lying to you everywhere you go / Turn to and put out all your strength of art and heart and brain / And like the Mary Ellen Carter rise again."

Stan Rogers

Table of Contents

Introduction

Allen Clarke's Adventures in Investing is about creating wealth for yourself. But don't worry—you don't need a computer and web access to benefit from this advice. Although you will find several useful references to web sites for when you finally enter the new economy, there are lots of valuable insights within the book that don't require the web. The e-commerce Internet connection is simply the use of the Internet to access and process further information that will assist you in wealth creation—no more, no less. If I had written this book 20 years ago I could have included the Dewey decimal and Library of Congress numbers to aid you in your library searches.

The real value of the Internet is the democratization of information—by that I mean that access to information can no longer be controlled by a small financial elite. Today, knowledgeable investors can access basically the same information as quickly as professional investors can—and in many cases faster because they can focus the research to their specific requirements. There is no doubt that the Internet has leveled the playing field when it comes to access to information, yet information remains open to an infinite number of interpretations and actions related to its use. We hope that this book will help you take advantage of it and create wealth with or without web access. However, throughout the book you will find references to various web sites that you can visit for more information or for further analysis.

"The lack of money is the root of all evil."
George Bernard Shaw

The first stock I ever owned was Husky Oil E warrants. I bought it in the mid-1970s from a Wood Gundy broker in Kingston and it immediately increased in value, and within a week I sold it for a nice profit. That made it look all too easy. No one should be this lucky on his or her first trade. No matter, I was hooked. Throughout the late 1970s I bought and sold stocks in my account. I deliberately use the term account here rather than portfolio because it was just an account full of unrelated stocks, which, as you will learn, does not constitute a portfolio. It wasn't until 1990, after I had left the brokerage industry for the trust industry, that I was properly introduced to the concept of portfolio construction. But that's Chapter 3.

Over the years, my account grew to a reasonable size, principally because I kept adding cash and not due to any real success resulting from the investing or trading activity. Surprisingly over that period, no one ever counseled me about the importance of creating a proper portfolio. As my account grew, we just took larger positions in a few stocks, the last of which was my biggest percentage loss, Pittston Coal.

In 1980, an opportunity arose for a career change and becoming a broker seemed the obvious new direction. I arranged for a couple of interviews with national Toronto-based firms: Wood Gundy in the morning and McLeod Young and Weir in the afternoon. A family friend, a professor of economics at Queen's University, recommended McLeod, with the added advice to "stay away from the bond market." Who knew that this was just two years before the beginning of the greatest bull market in bonds ever, lasting 17 years from 1983 to the end of the century. Certainly neither of us. By noon I had received a job offer from Wood Gundy and was considering canceling the McLeod appointment and heading home, but luckily reason prevailed.

That afternoon, McLeod also offered me a job, but more importantly I met with their head of sales. Now I'm in the corner office. We all know what that means. Well, at the time, I didn't, but in 15 short minutes, he had convinced me that North America was on the verge of the greatest economic expansion it had ever known. Further, he proposed that since the expansion would be resource based and in particular oil based, Canada, with its pipeline construction and its preponderance of oil, was perfectly positioned to get more than its fair share. What's more, only McLeod had the right position for me to fully participate in the market. It was an epiphany. I left his office convinced that the brokerage industry was the place to be and that McLeod was the right firm for me. In 15 short minutes he had me believing just what he wanted me to believe, which pretty much explains why he was head of sales!

In retrospect, my decision to leave a tenured teaching position at a Canadian college and enter an industry mired in a 10-year bear market was a gutsy move. Regardless, that 15-minute meeting and my subsequent decision have turned out to be the most pivotal events of my working career.

Today, there aren't many people in the financial industry who were here during the 1970s. In fact, a disquieting fact is that very few people in the industry today have ever experienced a bear market. The 1970s were the Kodiak of bear markets—the dark years. The market literally moved sideways for 10 years. Most brokers also held a second job, which under normal circumstances is not permitted by securities commissions. However, many of the brokerages' CEOs and presidents sought permission from the exchanges for their brokers to accept additional employment. After all, the phone seldom rang in the office and when it did, it was your spouse asking you to pick up milk on your way home from work.

The 1970s were the antithesis of the 1980s, however, and few people were prepared for the excitement. But this change didn't happen overnight. The 1980s were slow to show their true potential. The first couple of years looked like more of the same and then the bull woke up from his long sleep, but not without a few uneasy moments along the way. Today, most people believe that a prolonged sideways market move as characterized by the 1970s couldn't happen

The Dow 1970 to 2000

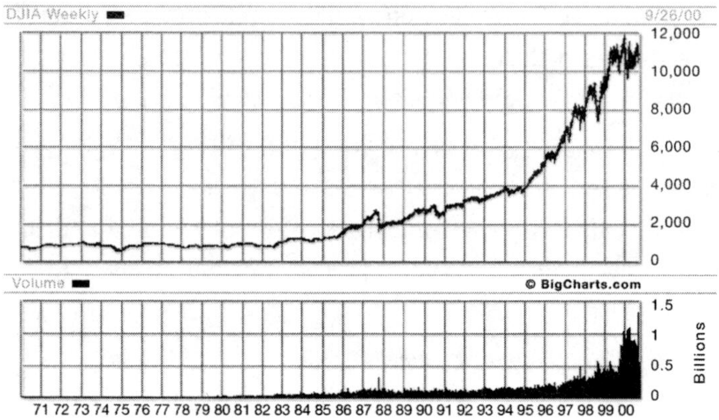

www.BigCharts.com

again. Well, not everyone. In a November 1999 article in *Fortune* magazine entitled "Mr. Buffett on the Stock Market," Warren Buffett argues just that point. He states that the markets are not always linked to value and that these periods of imbalance can persist for long periods. The Dow was 874.12 on December 31, 1964, and 875 on December 31, 1981. Yet, during this 17-year period, the GDP of the U.S. rose by some 370%; meanwhile, the Dow went nowhere. Buffett suggests that with continued inflation of 2% and real rates of returns of 4%, a 6% rate of return is more realistic, and like the period from 1964–81, we could experience times in which the markets simply don't appreciate.

As it turns out, the McLeod head of sales was absolutely right—but for all the wrong reasons. In fact, it wasn't 10 years but rather 20 years of unprecedented growth; it was not driven by resource development, and pipeline construction played a minor role. Regardless, the brokerage industry was the best place to be in the 1980s and McLeod was a great choice of firms. To me, this defines luck: being in the right place for all the wrong reasons.

To set the stage when I entered the financial industry, cast your mind back to the early 1980s.

Market Gurus

In the spring of 1980 the Dow Jones Industrial Average was in the 700s. Technical analysis was at its zenith, and the most-followed analyst on Wall Street, Joseph Granville, using his theory of on-balance volume (OBV), was calling for a massive pullback of more than 400 points to below the 500 level. On June 25, 1981, with the Dow at 996, Granville enters the gallery of the New York Stock Exchange and, amid boos and hisses, gave a big thumbs-down to the mass of traders on the exchange floor below. Within a year, the Dow Jones goes through 1,000 like corn through a goose and Granville, whom I believe is still short, was seldom heard of again.

Granville's most significant and enduring contribution is undoubtedly on-balance volume, which is used in technical analysis. It is a line constructed by measuring each day's volume and subtracting it, if the price is down, or adding it, if the price is up. It is based on the belief that volume is a precursor to a change in price trend. Increasing volume equates to increasing price and vice versa. However, the most useful aspect of OBV is as a predictor of a change in the price trend. A stock whose price is falling on increasing volume may signal a buying opportunity or, I believe, may be a useful indicator of a potential price drop. When a stock is rising on decreasing volume, it indicates in advance a falling stock price. Even today, many money managers apply various management styles; in particular, momentum managers still rely heavily on OBV to time their selling of stocks and some value managers use a similar process to time purchases and sales.

THE GRANVILLE MARKET LETTER
P.O. Drawer 413006, Kansas City, MO 64141
1 year, 46 issues, $250 U.S.

Meanwhile, in Ottawa, I was working for McLeod Young and Weir after 11 years as a college teacher, and trying to deal with the bear market of the early 1980s: mortgage rates of 19%; Canada Savings Bonds yielding 19.5%; Canada 9 1/2 01 bonds trading at near 50 cents on the dollar yielding 18%; a 14% Transalta Preferred that no one wanted to buy; the price of oil was predicted to be on its way to $75 a barrel; and Dome Petroleum was $100. And if that weren't enough, I had an office manager who was a loyal Granville follower and had all his accounts shorting the market, and who was breathing down my neck to get all my clients to short the market as well. As I said, the Dow goes through 1,000 like corn through a goose. At that point, two senior guys from Toronto arrive in the office one morning; by noon the manager is gone, and I am managing the Ottawa office of McLeod Young and Weir—the same office that E. P. Taylor had run for McLeod many years earlier. Nice footsteps for a 36-year-old ex-college teacher to follow.

What to do? No problem. The previous manager was short, and now he's gone. So, I go long. On October 11, 1982, the Dow permanently climbed above 1,000. I announce to the entire office that in their lifetimes they would never see 1,000 on the Dow again and that we had better get our clients into the market while we can. Interestingly, this was the Dow's fourth run at 1,000—first on November 14, 1972, then on March 11, 1976, again on November 20, 1980, and finally on October 11, 1982. You already know the rest of the story. The Dow went from 824 on January 1, 1980, to over 11,497 on December 31, 1999, almost a fourteenfold increase in 20 years, and the TSE 300 moved from 1,813 on January 1, 1980, to 8,413 on December 31, 1999, only a 4.7-fold increase. Life's sweet (sweeter if you've been in the U.S. markets rather than in the Canadian markets, but sweet nonetheless). Nothing like being in the right place at the right time, or the right place at the right time for the wrong reasons.

If I learned one thing from this incident, it is that nothing is as dangerous to your career as being on the wrong side of the market or out of the market. If your clients don't get you, the guys in Toronto will. Never forget that you can't fight the markets.

Now that Granville had been discredited, along came Robert Prechter and the Elliott Wave Theory, and again the world marched to a new pied piper. Named after Ralph Nelson Elliott, he concluded, based on observations in nature, that all human behavior, including the movement of the stock market, could be predicted by observing and identifying sets of predictable and repetitive waves. The idea was first published in the 1939 edition of *Financial World* and reignited by Prechter and Frost in their 1978 publication "Elliott Wave Principle."

In October 1987, with the Dow at 2,639 on the first day of the month, Prechter failed to warn his clients of the October 20 pullback to 1,616, although this point was hotly contested at the time. That's just short of a 40% correction in a matter of days. To put it in perspective today with the Dow at 11,000, that equates to a 4,200+ pullback over a two- to three-day period, and on the TSE at 10,000 it equates to a 3,800+ pullback. Then Prechter announced that he was actually short all along, and that his followers just hadn't interpreted his signals correctly. He remained short as the market climbed to new highs and kept going. Discredited and bruised, he sent all his subscribers a book of Japanese haiku poetry and disappeared to some Caribbean island to contemplate his navel, leaving all the technical guys rudderless and adrift.

THE ELLIOTT WAVE FORECAST
P.O. Box 1618, Gainesville, GA 30503
Monthly, 1 year, $228 U.S.

"The best time to invest is when you have money."
Sir John Templeton

Amid this confusion, Sir John Templeton, then just John Templeton, calmly announced that he expected to see the Dow close above 10,000 by the end of the century. Most people politely dismissed his proclamation as bravado in the face of massive uncertainty. Interestingly, it seems he was slightly low on the number.

After the Granville and Prechter fiascoes, you'd think that technical analysis had been dealt a mortal blow. But no, for a short time after that, the void was filled by Fibonacci, an obscure twelfth-century mathematician. Any port in a storm. He probably sat up in his grave, surprised as anyone that he was in vogue again after an 800-year hiatus—the new messiah of Wall Street. His theory was premised on the idea that certain numbers are intrinsically more favorable than others for the market. The Fibonacci era was short-lived, however, and technical analysis has not recovered from this string of embarrassing gurus.

Keep in mind that the early 1980s were a different time. Technical analysis was at its zenith. All major brokerage firms devoted a significant portion of their training and research budgets to technical analysis. No new broker of this era graduated without a complete working knowledge of point and figure charting, or on-balance volume, and the ability to recognize a double bottom on a chart when they saw one. Today, however, momentum managers are the surviving technical players.

During that period, value investing wasn't the populist cornerstone that it is today. Warren Buffett didn't step forward to do intellectual battle with the technical gurus of his day. This wasn't comparable to the great British evolution debates of the nineteenth century between Darwin and Huxley. Rather, the technical giants were left unchallenged, except by the conflicting realities of the markets. To quote Lord Byron: "The Assyrian came down like a wolf on the fold," or, in this case, the realities of the godless markets, in due course, laid them to waste.

The present-day epicenter of value investing is Warren Buffett's company, Berkshire Hathaway. In January 1980 it traded at $315 a share, and in March 1999 it traded above $80,000 a share. That's an annual rate of return over the past 19 years of more than 30%. The past few years, however, have not been kind to value investors. In early 2000 Berkshire Hathaway investors saw a full 50% pullback in price to the low-$40,000 range.

And then there were Dr. Doom and Dr. Gloom—Paul Volcker and Henry Kaufman—and every Thursday afternoon during the late 1980s they made the financial world stand still and every trader hold their breath, awaiting the money-supply number. Money supply became the newest idol to be both feared and worshiped with religious regularity. Clients would stop me on the streets of Ottawa and ask about the money-supply number that week and whether there was a revision in the previous week's number—as if it mattered to their lives and as if we really understood what it meant. In retrospect, most of the numbers were eventually revised anyway so how could the numbers have been so critical, or more importantly, how could you have profited by them? This is not dissimilar to today's preoccupation with quarterly earnings and the "earning season," although I want to believe that earnings are more important. Ten years from now preoccupation with quarterly earnings may seem as silly as money supply.

"Central bankers are brought up pulling the legs off ants."
Paul Volcker

Then the financial industry found comfort in a proliferation of product developments, each producing its whole new profusion of products: preferreds with all sorts of bells and whistles, such as retractions or extensions, government guarantees or attached warrants; mortgaged-backed securities (MBS); stripped coupons; deferred sales charges; hedge funds; and futures. This phenomenon culminated in 1994, when David Bowie securitized the revenue stream from his music, including "The Rise and Fall of Ziggy Stardust and the Spiders from Mars," for U.S.$55 million of "Bowie's Bonds." Bowie took all the rights to his music and the projected cash flow from those rights and sold them in the form of a security, a bond, which reflected the worth and potential long-term royalty cash flow, so he would receive a large sum of cash immediately and in exchange for all future royalties on his music. In turn, the buyer would receive a bond and a continuing revenue stream based on future royalties. That had to be dogs living with cats.

What have I learned from all this? Gurus, soothsayers, forces, crises and visionaries come and go, but the value of the entire capital infrastructure in the world keeps increasing, and the markets, to reflect that appreciating asset, keep going up.

Most of these market pundits share a classic flaw—an obsessive belief in their ability to call short-term market moves. Many investors who profess to be true investors with long-term investment time frames become traders when they are tricked into following the preaching of market gurus who promise higher returns through short-term market timing. In reality, they introduce higher commission costs and more often than not sideline investors during significant market evaluations, leading to lower returns for investors, not to mention frustration and anxiety. Anyone who is a proponent of short-term market moves usually has ulterior motives that are not in your best interest as an investor, so beware!

What does this mean to you and me? Simply that the real risk is in not participating, not being in the market and not sharing in the wealth creation as an owner of capital. The problem with market timing is you must get out and then back in; to benefit you must be correct twice—and twice in a row. The real risk to the investor is not being in the market, but rather being out of the market.

Market Timing

Consider the following as case in point. In the summer of 1987, I received a call from a large client. "Sell everything," he insisted. "Did you read the article in *Time* magazine?" We sold as he requested, and in October, he was looking like a genius sitting in cash. Unfortunately, however, he still had to get back into the market to make money, and just like my manager seven years earlier when the Dow was at 700, this guy just couldn't bring himself to get back in. As a result, not only was any benefit of going to cash lost but so too was the opportunity to make money when the market resumed its long-term appreciation. If being right once is difficult, then being right twice in a row is virtually impossible. Remember: you have to get back in, and the negative mind-set that got you out is also likely to prevent you from getting back in on time. Trying to time short-term pullbacks in the market is a mug's game.

In retrospect, it would appear that the financial past and many of its great minds have turned out to be poor predictors of the financial future, particularly anyone attempting to predict short-term market moves for the purpose of trading in and out. This should make most of us uncomfortable, since many people count on the opposite to be true, in order to construct their own personal financial safety net. Out of this, there does seem to be one underlying truth that lays waste to much of the confusion: industrial growth creates wealth. The stock markets represent that wealth. Being in the market transfers that wealth to individuals, and that wealth has the ability to create opportunities—opportunities to compound wealth, to enhance personal circumstances and to keep promises.

The real substance of life today is embodied not in the promises we make, but in the promises we keep. The big promises such as "Don't worry, Mom, we'll take care of you," or "When you grow up, we'll be able to send you to university," or "When we retire, we'll be able to maintain our lifestyle and travel." All of these promises entail serious financial resources. The ability to fulfill these obligations and keep these promises requires new and unique skills.

Wealth Creation

Wealth creation occurs when you are able to have and accumulate investable assets, and when money works for you as opposed to you working for money. This is what I refer to as Opus 2 (that's Latin for the second work).

Often I hear accountants, lawyers, doctors or friends complaining about their incomes. They all have two things in common, beyond the fact that I am not overly sympathetic to their plight. First, they derive all their income from hourly billing, and second, they don't understand the Opus 2 concept. If your income results from the billing of your time, you're obviously restricted by the number of hours in the day and the value set by the market for an hour of that work. The same concept applies if you receive a fixed salary. However, if you were in manufacturing, you could increase sales and add new products, or if you were in retail you could open more stores or hire more salespeople. But when you're billing by the hour or on a fixed salary, you're stuck. This is definitely something to consider when you're deciding which path to take in college.

> "I want to get rich but I never want to do what there is to do to get rich."
>
> *Gertrude Stein*

To create real wealth, you must move beyond salaried cash flow. That's why I'm primarily interested in Opus 2, the second work, the period of your life when you have surplus cash flow to dedicate to investing. For most people, wealth creation can only occur if they are prepared to divert a portion of their income resulting from salary, commission or hourly billings to create an investment portfolio that is capable of producing its own additional reinvestable cash flow, which results in compounding. There is nothing as magical as money making money, which in turn makes more money.

Now some of you may be thinking about the lost opportunities of the bull market of the past two decades—"Gosh, I just missed a chance to participate in a fourteenfold increase in the equity market. Think about the wealth I could have created. What now?" First, you can't do anything about having missed the move over the past 20 years, so don't give it another thought. Furthermore, most of the people who actually worked in the industry didn't participate in the market during that period to the extent that they could have or should have. The future, however, is a different story and you can participate in the rest of the big Dow move to 40,000 and the TSE to 20,933.

Future Targets for the Dow and TSE

Which brings me to why I'm convinced that the Dow is inexorably moving towards the 40,000 level. The Dow has had good long-term rates of return (5-year 24.5%; 10-year 15.4%; 15-year 16.2%) as of December 31, 1999; and the broader-based S&P 500 even better (5-year 28.6%; 10-year 18.2%; 15-year 18.9%) as of December 31, 1999. If history simply repeated itself, the Dow could achieve the move from 11,497 at January 1, 2000, to 40,000 by duplicating its 19.51% rate of return over the past 6.99 years for the next 6.99 years, arriving at the exalted 40,000 level just before New Year's 2007 or thereabouts.

The TSE 300 has done very well compared to the Dow over the past year (47.4% compared to –4.8%) ending June 30, 2000. Over the longer time frame, however, the TSE has not fared nearly as well on the return side (5-year 16.9%; 10-year 10.5%; 15-year 11.7%), ending December 31, 1999. So if history repeated itself in Canada over the same 6.99-year time frame, with a rate of return of about 13.93% for that period, the TSE could make its move from 8,413 on January 1, 2000, to 20,933 by about New Year's 2007.

However, as mentioned, the year-to-date numbers ending June 30, 2000, are very poor for the Dow (–4.8%) and spectacular for the TSE (+47.4%), and have already placed these 2007 New Year's predictions at risk with the TSE 300 now above the 10,000 level. I would revise the return numbers a bit lower on the Dow and higher on the TSE, and adjust my TSE target to at least 30,000 and the Dow target short of 40,000 by early morning on January 1, 2007.

Using Warren Buffett's more conservative return number of 6% on January 1, 2007, the Dow should be at 17,277 and the TSE at 12,642.

The truth will undoubtedly be somewhere in between, but the overriding reality tells us that it will be higher—much higher. The TSE, at time of writing in late June 2000, was already over 10,000, no doubt on its way to 12,642 and beyond. I wonder which numbers—17,277 or 12,642 or 40,000 or 20,933 or 30,000—are good Fibonacci numbers? Time will tell.

I believe that Sir Wilfrid Laurier was off by 100 years in his prediction and that it is the twenty-first century that really belongs to Canada. I would not be surprised to see the TSE outperform the Dow over this period. I don't have any scientific basis beyond the feeling that we're just better positioned now to participate in the new economies, and that we're no longer the pure resource-based hewers of wood and drawers of water that Laurier envisioned. We are full participants in the growth engines of the twenty-first-century economy. I believe the TSE could outperform the Dow for the foreseeable future.

Two forces are at work that convince me that the wealth creation we've seen in the 1980s and 1990s is sustainable. First, the industrialized nations of the world continue to evolve from societies that exhibited surpluses of labor in the 1960s and 1970s and shortages of capital to societies that experience labor shortages and surpluses of capital. Every day, money pours into pension funds, RRSPs, 401ks and personal savings. There will be more than enough capital to power the continued growth of the economies and a sufficient surplus of capital to guarantee continued wealth creation. And there is demographic pressure. The boomers have fueled record consumption levels and soon they will do the same for savings and investing rates. We have not yet seen the full effect of the boomers on the growth of investing as we have in housing and retail consumption. Combined, these forces will create the second great wealth-creation opportunity of our lives.

Remember that over the past 20 years the Dow has increased fourteenfold from 824 to 11,497 for a 14% rate of return, while the

TSE has increased only 4.7-fold from 1,813 to 8,413 in the past 20 years for a 8% rate of return. But this time will be appreciably different. In the 1980s and 1990s, many boomers did not have disposable income to invest, so they missed the opportunity to create wealth outside their homes. This time, however, many boomers are in the Opus 2 phase of their lives and have the investable earnings to participate in this wealth creation. They're perfectly positioned for the rest of the ride to 40,000 and the next great wealth-creation opportunity. Remember the old days when billionaires were rare? On New Year's Day, 2007, you won't be able to swing a dead cat without hitting one. In 2000, *Forbes* estimates that there are more than 308 billionaires in the United States alone, and who knows how many more are lurking worldwide.

The world's richest man is Microsoft's Bill Gates at about $60 billion, followed by Oracle's Larry Ellison (or vice versa depending on their stock price), and third is Microsoft's cofounder Paul Allen. The world's richest woman is Helen Robson Walton, one of the heirs to the Sam Walton fortune, and Canada's richest man, Ken Thomson, ranked 18th worldwide with $16 billion.

Boomers and compounding wealth are the real reasons that the Dow is headed to 40,000 and the TSE to 20,933. The baby-boomer cohort comprises the 18 years from 1946 to 1964; at the turn of the century the oldest of this cohort is 54 and the youngest is 36. Knowing that the average age of a brokerage client is in the mid-fifties, one realizes that the boomers are just now entering the Opus 2 stage of their lives—that stage where they have surplus earnings that they can make available for investment purposes. We have seen the effects of boomers on industry production, job creation, housing prices and consumer spending, but we have yet to see the full weight of their propensity to invest. With the average boomer aged 46 and not yet at his or her peak investment age, there can be little doubt that we have not seen the end of this bull market.

Missing the two greatest market wealth-creation opportunities in your lifetime is just too sad to consider, so over the next few chapters we will provide you with the insights and skill sets to participate professionally in the next wealth creation, so you can keep those promises. We'll show you how to successfully ride the Dow to 40,000 and the TSE 300 to 20,933, so that sometime around January 1, 2007, you will have received your fair share.

"I've been rich and I've been poor, and rich is a lot better."
Bette Midler

1 "Failure to Read Further Can Be Financially Injurious"

"The thing always happens that you really believe in. The belief in a thing makes it happen."
Frank Lloyd Wright

This is not a book on how to beat Wall Street. It's a book for investors who have tried and come up short of their expectations, who have ventured into the uncertainties of the stock market with predictably uninspiring results. It will show you how to improve your odds of success with your investments.

Most investors unknowingly stack the deck against themselves. They make investment decisions that sabotage their chances, even before they start. In many cases, investors unknowingly expose themselves to undue levels of risk, resulting in loss of their investment capital and handicapping their capabilities for wealth creation right from the start. But even more alarming is that investors often miss out on opportunities for good returns because they do not know where to look for or how to properly construct an investment, and do not even recognize a realistic rate of return.

While there are no real mysteries to success, the best results, as in any venture, most often go to those who are experienced, disciplined and prepared. To avoid a costly learning process, fraught with financial misfortune and personal frustration, let's look at what successful professionals do, so you can leapfrog other investors on their heuristic journey. You'll also quickly learn that financial success has less to do with making a once-in-a-lifetime killing and more to do with developing the right attitude and a winning strategy.

This doesn't require a vast knowledge of the arcane mysteries of the inner workings of the stock markets, but rather an understanding of a few basic principles that have been learned the hard way by some of the most astute and successful investors in the world today.

"Eighty percent of success is showing up."
Woody Allen

Although Woody Allen's quotation might be the case for some adventures, it does not apply to investing, where lack of preparation is a formula for disaster. Furthermore, relying on common sense in the investment process is grossly overrated. In reality, many of the skills needed to become a successful investor are counterintuitive; that is, they actually go against common sense. It's a lot like learning to drive on an icy road—in which case you must teach yourself to turn in the direction of the slide. If you follow your instincts, common sense will put you in the ditch. This is often the case with investing. Common sense, based on past experiences totally unrelated to investing, can be dangerously misleading. In fact, some of the worst investors are professionals from other disciplines. Because of their status in their profession and the fact they are sought for counsel, they mistakenly believe that their professional skill sets will be appropriate to investing.

If you want to be a duck, you must walk like a duck and talk like a duck; if you want to manage money professionally and create wealth for yourself, you must do what professional money managers do. However, most of us fail to do this because we're unaware of what professional money managers actually do. As a result, many investors sabotage their financial success and are forced to settle for much less than they bargained for at the end of the day. You must prepare yourself for the task ahead, and the first step is to find out what the pros do. Read on.

"Chance favors the informed mind."
Louis Pasteur

The Cost of Retirement

It's 1984. I'm at my desk at the Ottawa office of McLeod Young and Weir and I receive a call from a friend, a broker in London, Ontario.

"Bill's gone," my friend says. "Made a big score in the commodities market and he's buying a dive shop in the Bahamas."

In disbelief, I ask, "How much did he make?"

"One point three million."

"That's enough?" I ask.

"I guess so, he's gone already."

So that's what it takes: $1.3 million. Well, I don't have it, so I return to my work, but I can't get the image of that dive shop out of my head. I am short some bonds and they're moving against me like Wellington at Waterloo. When you run a dive shop, things can go wrong in paradise too, I think, but it doesn't seem to make me feel any better. This might be because in the last five minutes I have lost enough money to buy a couple of dive shops in the Bahamas.

Fast-forward to 1998. A close friend of mine, a full-service broker, comes by the house. We start to discuss his work—probably because at that time I am not working. I'm washing the car. He starts to help. It's a guy thing.

"I've only got a few years left," he says.

In disbelief, I ask, "You're dying?"

"No, you idiot," he says. "It's my job."

We talk about how things are changing—the big banks, the cuts in payouts to brokers, the discounting, the discounters. "Gosh," he says, "twenty years of hard work and they're conspiring to push us out. If I had $3 million, I'd be gone."

So, I think to myself, the take-this-job-and-shove-it number has gone up to $3 million. Which leads to the real question: Have you ever really thought about how much money you might actually need to stop working?

For some of us, the number may be even more modest than the $3 million mentioned by my friend. For example, an article in a June 2000 issue of the *National Post* related the experience of a 36-year-old woman who had just retired. She had never earned more than $26,000 a year, had a net worth of $500,000, house included, and lived on a mere $10,000 a year. As remarkable as this is, when you read between the lines, it reveals a lifestyle and compulsion for thrift that few people could (or would want to) match. However, this example clearly illustrates the range of requirements that people have for the retirement of their dreams and that, with proper planning, retirement at age 55 to 60 is certainly possible. For most people, age 60 will be a far more realistic target than 55.

Before we get to the question of how to invest, which is covered in Chapters 3 and 4, and the conclusion, it is useful to figure out how much, like my friend, we will need to save. After the house and education, retirement is the big financial nut. For most of us, being able to retire at age 55 is a myth, and if we're not careful, there is even a risk that we will outlive our savings. In fact, it is probably more realistic to think of 60-plus as a retirement age, throw in some part-time work for added income and stop thinking of full retirement at age 55 right now.

Have you ever really thought about how much money you might actually need to retire, or how long you might live in retirement? Assuming that you and your spouse need $50,000 a year in pre-tax income to sustain your lifestyle and that you retire at 60 in good health, here's what it looks like:

The Canadian male is likely to live until age 78, while the average Canadian female should live until age 85. While that translates to an

18-year retirement period for the average guy, it equates to 25 years for the gal. But also consider that the average female is three years younger than her spouse. Therefore, if they retire together, when he is 60, this means a whopping 28-year retirement period for her.

> "If I knew I was going to live so long
> I would have taken better care of myself."
> *Mickey Mantle*

Did you know that Mickey Mantle hit 536 career home runs? His longest, and the longest home run ever measured to the spot where it landed, was 632 feet, and that was on October 9, 1960, at Tiger Stadium in Detroit.

To put this retirement period in perspective, just think back 25 years to where you were and what you were earning. Then ask yourself if you could live on those same annual earnings today. For example, in 1970, 30 years ago, my first full-time job was as a community college teacher earning $6,800 a year in Kingston and, at the time, it was a very good salary. A few years later I bought my first house in Kingston for $30,000. In 1998, the average Canadian family had an after-tax income of $49,626, and today about 10% of households have an income of $100,000 or greater. The average price of a house in midtown Toronto was $376,761 in early 2000. If you retire at age 55 to 60 and are in good health, this will give you a feel for what all this retirement stuff means to you financially over a 20- to 30-year period.

Women and Retirement

Assuming an average yield of 8%, which is a reasonable number, a couple needs, considering modest inflation, about $580,000 at retirement to cover the male, and $680,000 to cover his spouse (this takes into account CPI numbers of 2.3 over 1 year, 1.6 over 5 years and only 2 over the last 10 years). The additional requirements to secure a comfortable retirement for the usually younger and longer-living female are often overlooked, with the serious, unfortunate and often-unintended consequence of the woman outliving her money. Despite this, the number of pensioners who do not opt for continuing spousal benefits is alarming.

Yet, for women, who are generally believed to be more risk averse, there is yet another danger: the mistaken but prevalent belief that there is less risk in a fixed-income portfolio than in a properly diversified equity portfolio. But that's not what the math says. If a portfolio has a high fixed-income component, reducing the yield by just 1% to a yield of 7%, the cash requirement on retirement increases by $100,000 to $780,000. So you can imagine the enormous financial requirement if it were reduced further to 5% to 6%, which are the yields of today's guaranteed investment certificates. Clearly we must consider the life expectancy of the potentially longest-living spouse, typically the woman. I cannot explain why more pension plans do not make spousal benefits a requirement, since often the surviving spouse is left destitute at a period in her life where she is least capable of generating cash flow.

For further reading on this topic, refer to an interesting article in the fall 1994 edition of *Canadian Investment Review.* Entitled "How to Avoid Outliving Your Money" and written by Ho, Milevsky and Robinson, the article addresses the specific dangers facing women in terms of outliving their money as a result of holding portfolios with high fixed income and lower yields.

> "Women hold up more than half the sky."
> *Chinese proverb*

If you believe this proverb, you now realize that women also hold it up longer and at greater cost.

We have just come through an 18-year bull market in bonds, including the 19.5% Canada Savings Bond (CSB) issue in 1982, a period in which bond yields and returns on fixed income were exceptional. Unless interest rates go to zero, this is unlikely to continue and historic rates of return in fixed income, and bond funds, will not even remotely reflect the past. Actually, in Japan, interest rates have been at zero on overnight money. As a result, I'd be extremely wary of any financial advice about using your age as a guideline for the appropriate percentage of fixed income. This rule is based on the premise that if you're aged 50, then 50% of your money should be in fixed income; if you're 60, then it would be 60%; and so on. Unfortunately, this rule inadvertently and unnecessarily introduces the risk of outliving your money—especially when a properly diversified equity portfolio can mitigate this risk regardless of your age.

With these lofty funding requirements for the average Canadian to successfully retire at modest levels, it's not surprising that a recent survey suggests that 62% of Canadians now expect to continue working in retirement. More interestingly, this statistic fails to reveal whether respondents actually *know* that they may have to work or whether they simply *want* to work at some activity of their choice. In the United States today, you often see older people working at McDonald's. One can only guess whether such employment fulfills a social or financial need. Yet, in the U.S. media, the income gap that this employment revenue fills for older Americans is commonly referred to as "The Mac Gap."

Did you know that McDonald's is located in 110 countries worldwide and opens a new store every six hours? By the way, there are an average of 198 sesame seeds on every Big Mac bun.

Government Support

In the United States, the lack of commitment to retirement savings is at epidemic proportions; the personal saving rate hovered between 7% and 11% for over 30 years from the 1960s to early 1990s but is now below 1%. In August 1998 *The Economist* stated, "Americans have been on a spending binge, well beyond growth of their incomes." In fact, recent data show that Americans may be moving to negative savings, where they spend existing savings. This is undoubtedly related to the fact that in the United States there has been a 20-year stagnation of family incomes.

The median value of household financial assets in America in 1995 was $9,950 and, despite the prolonged bull market, by 1997, 40% of baby boomers had less than $10,000 in savings. Sixty percent of families have only one month of cash flow if they lose their jobs, and the next 20% had means for only 3.5 months. Evidently, retirement planning doesn't seem to be a priority for most Americans.

Now before we paint too bleak a picture, these numbers do not reflect what savings are going on by way of paying down mortgages or by way of appreciation within investment portfolios, yet I can't imagine that the average American's increased spending would be offset by these factors.

When Social Security was introduced in the United States in the early 1950s, the age to qualify was set at age 70—slightly above the average life expectancy of age 69 for average Americans at that time. Coincidence? Perhaps now that more Americans are living to collect the benefit, it is hardly surprising that governments worry about their ability to fund annuitants.

Canadians face an even more interesting problem with the Canada Pension Plan (CPP). Most Canadians believe that, like the corporate pensions they are familiar with, the government has put aside a pool of money to fund their requirement as they reach qualifying age. Few realize that only a small amount of money has been put aside—$40 billion or so—which falls far short of the $500 billion or so required to meet future obligations of Canada Pension Plan annuitants. This means that the additional funds must come from increased contributions by working Canadians. The contribution rate will eventually be raised by 9.9% in 2003 and, if all goes well, this would allow for the continuation of the existing level of benefits. It will be interesting to see whether the government has done the math correctly and if baby boomers have, in fact, paid for their own retirement or whether this responsibility will fall as a burden to the next generation and, if so, whether they will be willing to pay.

Because Canadians now live longer and healthier lives than ever before, retirement is not the low-cost sedentary lifestyle it once was. In fact, many retired persons find themselves spending the same amount in retirement as they did when they worked. It would be good to ask yourself how long you think you and your spouse will live, and what percentage of your present income you will need in retirement to do the things you would like. Assuming that you will need only 50% to 75% of your existing cash flow may not allow you to maintain your existing lifestyle.

Chart of life expectancy from Statistics Canada

Life expectancy at birth

	Both sexes	Males	Females	Difference
		Years		
Canada				
1920-22	59	59	61	2
1930-32	61	60	62	2
1940-42	65	63	66	3
1950-52	69	66	71	5
1960-62	71	68	74	6
1970-72	73	69	76	7
1980-82	75	72	79	7
1990-92	78	75	81	6
1990-92				
Newfoundland	77	74	80	6
Prince Edward Island	77	73	81	8
Nova Scotia	77	74	80	6
New Brunswick	78	74	81	7
Quebec	77	74	81	7
Ontario	78	75	81	6
Manitoba	78	75	81	6
Saskatchewan	78	75	82	7
Alberta	78	75	81	6
British Columbia	78	75	81	6

Source: Statistics Canada, Catalogue no. 82F0075XCB.

www.statcan.ca

The Role of the Home in Retirement

Knowing that more than 50% of Canadians have saved less than $30,000 for their retirement leaves me wondering what will happen when all these forces converge on baby boomers over the next few years. This statistic does not, however, address the equity that Canadians have built in their personal residences by paying down their mortgages. In Canada, just over 50% of homes have no mortgage, so this situation may not be as bad as it first seems. However, the real excitement will come when this mass of baby boomers who have counted on this home equity to fund late retirement all try to access that equity either through reverse mortgages or the outright sale of their homes within relatively the same period of time. This has the potential to create a buyers' market and greatly reduce the liquidity and value of these homes. Reverse mortgages involve encumbering your house based on its value while also living in it, to receive a monthly cash flow that is constantly eating away at the value you have built in your home. The trick is to not outlive the cash-flow stream based on the constantly dwindling equity remaining in your home. Reverse mortgages have not proven popular in Canada since even banks don't like to evict elderly persons from their own homes when they outlive the equity that they worked a lifetime to create. However, watch for reverse mortgages to make a comeback as retired people face limited funding options.

When is your RRSP too small?

It will be more interesting to watch for those who have successfully planned and invested than for those who haven't. This leads me to the next issue, which is unique to Canada: that is, with the Canadian social net and the income clawback, when are Canadians better off to have saved and at what point should they have spent everything?

The answer to this question is simple. How much will you be able to save and where do you plan to save it? To get the point across, let's deal in round numbers.

If you're a single person aged 65 and you've saved nothing in your RRSP and have no additional earned income, you can expect to receive from the government:

- $5,000 Old Age Security (OAS),
- $6,000 Canada Pension Plan (CPP is determined by the period a person works and contributes, and can vary from zero to $9,000 per year),
- $3,000 Guaranteed Income Supplement (GIS) and
- a $1,000 tax credit, for a total of $15,000 (varies by province).
- Since only $11,000 is taxable, the taxes are almost nil and your after-tax income is almost the full $15,000.

If you're in the same situation but have managed to save $50,000 in an RRSP that generates $5,000 of additional earned income, you can expect to receive:

- $5,000 of earned income from the RRSP,
- $5,000 OAS,
- $6,000 CPP,
- only $500 GIS and
- a $1,000 tax credit, for a total of $17,500 (varies by province).
- Now, $16,000 is taxed and the taxes are about $1,200, leaving you with $16,300 after-tax.

This means that for every $1 in RRSP income, you will lose 50 cents of GIS benefits and pay 24 cents in taxes, so you will be receiving only 26 cents after tax. This is not as bad for a married person because there is not as much GIS. However, the bottom line is that there is no point in having a small amount of RRSP income from your RRSP that results in a small taxable income after age 65 when CPP, OAS and GIS start.

This is not to suggest, however, that you should not save or not have an RRSP, as some financial pundits have suggested. It simply means that you should start early, save a lot and invest wisely so that your RRSP is huge. But if you can't get your RRSP substantially above $50,000, you should save outside the RRSP or pay out the RRSP in the years leading up to age 65, so you will enter retirement with investment income, not RRSP income.

Income tax was introduced in Canada on April 24, 1917, as a "temporary" measure to fund a $600-million debt resulting from Canada's participation in World War I. It was introduced by Prime Minister Robert Borden and then Minister of Finance Sir Thomas Wright as the temporary "War Tax Upon Income" bill.

Relying on Inheritance

Now, let's address those readers who have been smugly sitting back and saying, "So what? I've got a big inheritance coming." To them, I would advise: I wouldn't be too sure. In 1995, Stephen M. Pollan and Mark Levine wrote what I consider to be one of the most insightful financial pieces in some time: *Die Broke*. These authors propose that a good life beats a good death and there are good reasons why parents should spend rather than bequeath their wealth.

Dying broke is a philosophy of living, not dying. It deals with quality of life—your life and your children's lives. Bequeathing a large inheritance weakens your children's desire to compete and shifts their focus to your dying more than your living. However, good financial deeds such as paying off your grandchild's student loan, putting a down payment on a starter home for your newly married son or daughter, or giving your son or daughter seed capital to start his or her own business helps them at a stage in life where that support means the most and when it has the greatest effect. It's this timing that can bring you and them the greatest pleasure.

"People don't have the fortunes left to them in that style nowadays; men have to work and women to marry money. It's a dreadfully unjust world."
Louisa May Alcott

My parents paid for my education and as a result I graduated from university debt free. By today's standards, it wasn't a lot of money, but it meant a lot to me, and it made a big difference in my life. In later life my parents continued to save. They didn't vacation much and they didn't often travel, because they were determined to create an inheritance. I recently received my inheritance, but I would have preferred the stories.

Baby boomers waiting around for the big score are likely to be disappointed. A 1993 U.S. survey suggested that only 42% of people with a living parent believed that they would receive an inheritance and, of those who did, only 24% thought it would be greater than $50,000. A mid-1980s Canadian study revealed that while the previous generation believed that building an inheritance was an appropriate goal, the current generation felt they would need their money for their own retirement. In one generation, the inheritance as a valued goal seemed to evaporate. As a result, in most cases it is imprudent to have a financial plan that relies on an inheritance.

And even if an inheritance exists, it is likely to come too late. If your parents became parents in their early twenties, you and your spouse could also be retired or certainly in your fifties before both parents pass away and leave you an inheritance. All four of you could be living in a trailer park in Florida, 20 miles from the beach, trying to decide whether 4:30 p.m. is too soon to go for the all-you-can-eat-catfish early-bird special dinner at Billy Bob's.

What's even more alarming is that if your parents live long and healthy lives, they could actually spend all their money, which includes using the equity in their home, to fund their extended retirement or be in no position to leave you an inheritance. Not to put an even more dire spin on this, but should your parents fail to have saved sufficiently in order to properly fund their retirement, you can be held financially responsible. In Ontario, there are parent-support laws and you, the children (not the state), could be responsible to take care of your parents financially, if they should need financial support. This is likely not a cost that you have factored into your financial plans. It would be prudent to discuss with your parents the potential need for you to help with their retirement. Waiting for your parents to die so you can skate your own finances on side is a very poor strategy.

The Risk of Outliving Your Money

Retirement is all about risk—not so much investment risk, but the risk of underfunding; in essence, the risk of outliving your money. But before we begin our discussion of risk, let's do away with one old adage: the greater the risk, the greater the reward. In fact, an ill-constructed portfolio often increases risk to investors and constrains the ability of the portfolio to generate good returns. You can unknowingly increase your risk of loss to capital and reduce your opportunity for returns—and many investors do just that.

This goal of maximum return and minimum risk is intrinsic in modern portfolio design, and is one of the pillars of modern portfolio theory that we will discuss in Chapter 4.

When it comes to financial planning, you can't swing a dead cat without hitting someone preaching about risk, standard deviation, Sharpe ratios or betas. Offer $100 and most of these evangelists couldn't identify a Sharpe ratio from a '56 Chevrolet. It's part of the mystique of financial planning to create this element of danger and in the process to drive the frightened client into the planner's comforting arms. Granted, financial planners can provide a very important service to investors by defining goals, building successful investment plans or investment portfolios and helping clients sift through the vast range of financial products, but using risk-centered approaches puts serious limitations on the process before it even begins. With almost 2,000 mutual funds alone, the valuable role of the planner in product selection should not be underestimated.

But if clients don't understand the question of risk, why ask it at all? I would argue that clients are better off not restricting their initial planning process, particularly with flawed information. To most planners, risk tolerance means allowing clients to determine the asset mix and the return rates at the beginning of the process, based on the assumption that higher returns are more risky and more fixed income is less risky. Most clients are ill equipped to deal with such questions. A better approach would be to run the retirement calculations with historically conservative return data, which will give clients a good feel for the probabilities of achieving their financial goals. Then, when clients can see the effects of any adjustments to the retirement goals, they will be in a better position to intelligently alter any of the key elements of their plan. The best way for clients to deal with the financial planning process is not to address risk tolerances but rather to assess the probability of meeting their financial goals.

Investment Risk

To me, risk comprises two basic elements: loss of capital and loss of opportunity for returns, not the usual reference to volatility. Such losses can result in even more serious exposure to risk among investors that is seldom realized until it is too late—the risk that they will not meet their financial goals and will outlive their money.

Risk really is a four-letter word, to quote George Hartman. Improperly communicated, from the beginning it restricts your investment strategy and greatly decreases your probability of success. Dealing with risk initially places restraints on the planning process before it begins and fails to deal with the all-important financial probabilities that will become realities in the future. Risk is not the overriding consideration in financial planning. Probability is. The ethereal elements of risk are not a good basis for investor planning. Rather, the hard realities of the investor's financial situation should dictate the course of action, and the outcome should be expressed in the more understandable terms of probabilities. The use of risk analysis has led to investment decisions that have created false comforts and misdirection in the financial planning process.

Risk is secondary to your goals. How you construct your portfolio is not determined by how you feel about risk but by the physical parameters of your situation, such as how much time you've got left to save, how much you can save, how much you'll need when you retire, how much you have to start with, and so on.

> "And the trouble is, if you don't risk anything, you risk even more."
>
> *Erica Jong*

Age is undoubtedly the main factor in this equation. In many cases, it comes down to time, not risk. If you're age 45 and have accumulated a fair amount of capital and your financial targets are in sight, then you can choose a slightly less aggressive portfolio. However, if you're age 60 or 70 and you still need a decent return to live on, your investment strategy will be determined by these circumstances—not by whether you feel comfortable with volatility and risk. Despite popular theories that attach undue importance to risk and your ability to handle it, if you are to maintain your lifestyle, whether you like risk becomes irrelevant.

For example, suppose you don't like risk and you are 50 years old. If you want to retire at age 60, you've either got to save a lot of money every year or be prepared to assume a more aggressive portfolio than you would like. And if you're older than 50 and in the same position, you're out of luck because you've put yourself in the riskiest position of all. That is, you've already taken on a lot more risk by waiting too long to begin the process and time is no longer on your side. You simply won't have enough capital to see you through your retirement or perhaps your savings are tied up in low-yield fixed-income investments such as GICs. Whatever the case, you've unknowingly added risk to your situation, even though you thought you were doing the opposite.

That's why your level of comfort with risk is irrelevant. At the end of the day, your investment strategy is determined by the physical parameters of your financial situation—not whether you feel comfortable with risk. Unfortunately, your alternative is to be prepared to simply run out of money or to work long beyond your anticipated retirement age.

It's a lot like the traveler who contacts his travel agent in Halifax and tells the agent that he must be in Vancouver that evening but doesn't like to fly. However, at this point his level of comfort with flying has absolutely nothing to do with his dilemma. If he wants to get to Vancouver that evening, he has no other option but to board the plane, pull down the window shades, go to sleep and wake up when he gets there. Any discussion of bus or train travel would be futile because it would fail to meet the traveler's main need—to travel across Canada that day. The same rationale applies to discussions of risk tolerance, particularly when a well-crafted investment portfolio can safely get you where you want to go financially.

This raises other issues about risk and how we short-change ourselves by trying to avoid it. If you put too much of your money into fixed-income investments such as GICs and CSBs, or design a portfolio that produces less yield than necessary, your savings will be depleted much sooner than you bargained for. This represents a far bigger risk than the risk of losing your money in a properly constructed portfolio. A highly diversified equity portfolio is less volatile than a portfolio with a high fixed-income component, and if a portfolio with a large amount of fixed income falls short of your goals, you have exposed yourself to the ultimate risk—poverty at an age when you have no earning capacity.

Don't worry—if you still have concerns about risk, there are ways to mitigate it, principally through diversification. However, like many other things in life, unless you're properly trained and equipped, you can't do it well. This also necessitates a discussion on performance and how capital preservation goes hand in hand with yields and returns. We'll deal fully with diversification and capital preservation in Chapter 3.

"There are two rules to investing.
Rule #1, don't lose money. Rule #2, don't forget rule #1."
Warren Buffett

Risk Is for Older People

I'd like to add a third rule to Buffett's recommendations, one that has got me into trouble a few times, but one I strongly believe in: "Risk is for old guys and gals." Yes, if you're going to take risk, it's most appropriate for older experienced persons with money, not for young people beginning the investment process.

Let's say you're 65 years old and have saved $800,000. Your house is paid for and you have no debt. You want to take a $30,000 flier on a junior oil company drilling in Indonesia. You've earned the right. It won't affect your lifestyle either way, whether, as they say in the business, the investment goes up or blows up. It will, however, annoy any offspring who might be waiting for that inheritance and this is exactly where I got into trouble. However, if you're 30 years old and you take a flier on a software company that turns into vaporware, this is different—very different and very wrong. Taking this kind of risk with capital, at a critical developmental stage in your wealth-building years, before you have sufficient capital to benefit from compounding, is totally inappropriate.

To illustrate my point, consider the following scenario. Let's take two 30-year-old investors, each with $30,000, and adding $10,000 to

$ 523,482 The Real Cost of Early Risk to Capital

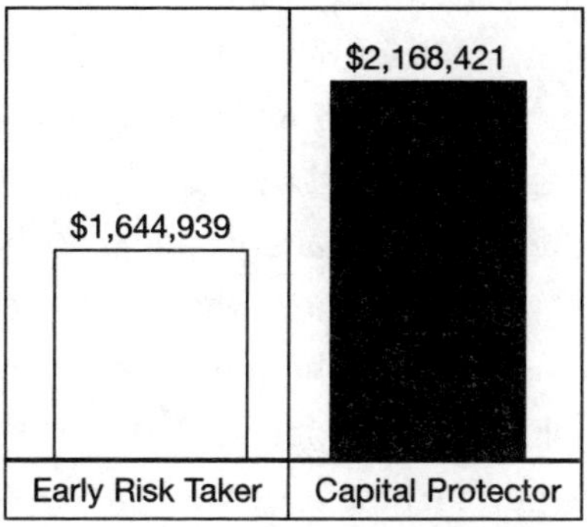

the investment a year at a 10% return and retiring at 60. The trader risks the $30,000 and loses, and then resumes saving. He or she retires with $1,644,939. The investor doesn't risk the $30,000 capital. He or she just keeps investing and retires with $2,168,421. So what seemed to be a simple $30,000 mistake actually becomes a $523,482 mistake. And it gets even worse because this $523,482 equates to an additional $61,487-a-year income over a 20-year retirement.

Compounding is your friend. Capital depreciation is the enemy. And risk is for old guys and gals.

> "I don't know the seven wonders of the world, but know the eighth and it's compound interest."
>
> *Rothschild*

Hewlett Packard 17B Calculator

To understand whether you are indeed properly funding your retirement, you must be able to do a future value calculation. If you give a man a fish, you feed him for a day; if you teach a man to fish, you feed him for life. The same principle applies to financial plans and future value calculations. Learn to do your own future value calculations and you'll have meaningful input into the planning and checking of your financial future. So this is a good time to become familiar with the Hewlett Packard 17B and the future value calculation.

Dave Packard and Bill Hewlett founded Hewlett Packard (HP) in 1934. They began in this one-car garage at 367 Addison Avenue, Palo Alto, California, now a designated historic site, with $538 in working capital. HP's first product was the resistance-capacity audio oscillator HP 200A, and their first client was Walt Disney, who ordered eight oscillators (HP 200B) for the production of the movie *Fantasia*. HP now has more than 85,000 employees worldwide.

Your first step is to go out and purchase a Hewlett Packard 17B calculator. Don't be talked into anything else. Look up the section on future values in the instruction booklet and learn how to do the calculation. Everything you need to know to put you and your spouse on the right RRSP track is embodied in this future value calculation.

It isn't complicated; only five variables are involved: time to retirement in years (N or number of years), the annual RRSP contribution levels (PMT or payment), how much money you have in your RRSPs now (PV or present value) and the rates of return you expect to get (I or interest rate).

Use a single-digit return (i.e., 8%) if you have a properly diversified portfolio with a good percentage of equities. Lately, some investors have experienced remarkable double-digit rates of return and have grown to expect, if not demand, these levels of return going forward. The most worrisome part of this phenomenon is investors' mistaken belief that such returns are principally the result of investor intellect. Yet, these double-digit returns lack long-term historic foundation, have been isolated to specific asset classes and are often the result of a concentration of a few stocks within the indices that represent those asset classes.

> "Don't confuse brains with a bull market."
>
> *Humphrey Neill*

Be realistic about the rates of return and generous with the amount of cash you believe you need on the first day of retirement (FV). This should be about 12.5 times what you think your pre-tax annual needs will be, assuming an 8% rate of return. Don't forget to use the minus (–) sign for your PMT and PV values.

Combine both your own and your spouse's RRSP contributions for the PMT value and both your present RRSP assets for the PV value. This will give you a combined retirement nest egg value—the FV.

Don't worry about pre-tax or after-tax. Just think pre-tax so if you presently need a pre-tax income of $75,000 to live on, calculate to match for a pre-tax cash flow of $75,000, and if you make a pre-tax RRSP contribution of $10,000 knowing that you will receive a tax-canceling tax refund, again simplify it by just thinking pre-tax dollars. Your financial planner or accountant can give you a more sophisticated analysis as you move closer to retirement and if your time frame allows it.

Take the sum of your nest egg, the FV, and take 8% of this as your pre-tax retirement income. This assumes an 8% rate of return and no use of principal. Not only is this conservative, but also by not touching the principal, you'll leave an inheritance and avoid having to predict when you will die.

As rudimentary as this is, as you play with the calculations, you'll develop a good understanding of the future value of money and the serious effects of retirement age, returns and contribution. By increasing your retirement age (N), you'll get a feel for the effect and the importance of working one more year. Or if you calculate the nest egg value (FV) when you turn 50 or 55, you'll see how this is not a realistic target for most people. Let's be careful: just because you can do the math doesn't mean you're there yet. Remember Warren Buffett's wise words, and recognize your limits.

> "When you have a horse that can count to 10, you have a remarkable horse, not a remarkable mathematician."
>
> *Warren Buffett*

When I was a senior executive with Central Guaranty Trust, one of my perks was a $5,000 financial plan, including life insurance inheritance planning and much more. However, spending $100 to buy the HP 17B and learning to operate it or using one of the many online calculators, listed below, that are based in the same future value calculation, will give most people a sound check of their retirement plans.

Now you're in a position to periodically check how well you're doing and generate some realistic financial scenarios. While it is reassuring to have the HP 17B and the flexibility of knowing how to do your own calculations, the following web sites also offer iterations of this future value calculator:

www.opus2direct.com/planner2.html
www.forbes.com/tool/html/toolbox.asp?category=calculators
www.independentfinancial.on.ca/calculators.htm
www.searchingweb.com/tools/calculators.shtml

It is still wise to seek professional investment help, particularly with respect to investment portfolio design and product selection, either by going direct, using WRAP or asset-allocation products where the manufacturer has delivered the investment portfolio through the product design, or by consulting a broker or planner. This raises one of the most interesting issues in the delivery of financial products today: who is responsible for adding value and what should the consumer pay for it?

The Value in Portfolio Design

In the past, the broker chose the stocks and bonds, while the planner chose the mutual funds and did most, if not all, the work to construct the portfolio. For that service, the broker traditionally received a gross annual trading commission rate of about 2.5%, of which he kept 50% or about 1.25%. The planner traditionally received an initial commission of 5.0% to 6.0% and a trailer of 0.5%, or again about a

2.5% annual gross commission rate, but unlike the broker, he or she kept 80% or about 2.0%. Today these numbers are facing increasing consumer pressure and, while moving lower, still amount to 1% or more annually. Over the life of your investment, this amounts to hundreds of thousands of dollars that otherwise would have directly enhanced the performance of your investments.

Today, however, with WRAP products, fund-to-fund mutual funds and direct asset-allocation tools, product construction is no longer done by the broker or planner, but by the corporation. This brings up the obvious question: what is the role of the broker and planner today, and what is the value of this service? Most would agree that the role of portfolio construction is better and more uniformly executed by the corporation. This leaves the brokers and planners to redefine their roles, which, for now, have shifted to those of problem-solvers and introduction services. While these new roles may seem diminished in value compared to the old role centered on portfolio construction, they have evolved as important and key client services in the proper execution of financial plans. The clear benefit to consumers can result from their unwillingness to continue to pay previous commission levels for these new roles by going direct or negotiating more favorable fee structures. These reduced fees are immediately reflected in better returns.

In the 1950s, Betty Crocker was faced with a similar problem when the company introduced its premixed cake mixes. What was a mother to do? If the corporation did all the work, the cake would no longer be perceived as "homemade." In a stroke of genius, Betty Crocker deliberately left out the eggs, leaving mother with a key role to play in the construction process, so when Sunday dinner rolled around the cake was still considered "homemade." Look for the financial industry to adopt a similar position with its corporately constructed managed products.

The real additional cost of the broker or planner services can be significant over time. To an average 30-year-old, making the $13,500 RRSP contribution until retirement at age 60, in a 10% return environment, the additional 1% of fees amounts to an additional cost of $296,330, a cost that otherwise would translate into higher returns and greater savings to clients.

$296,330.37 The Real Cost of Higher Fees

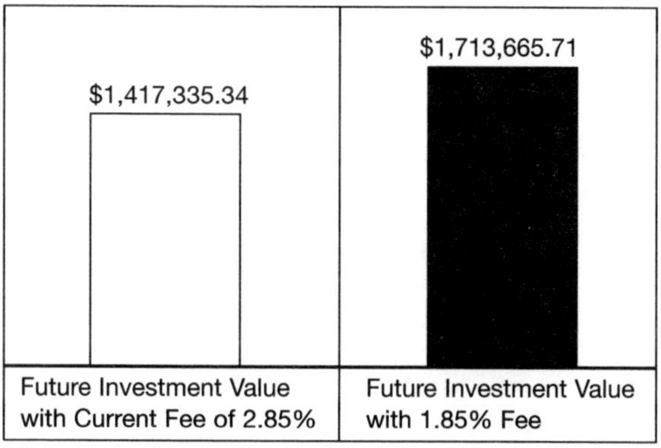

In the United States more than 40% of mutual funds are sold direct, resulting in lower costs for investors. In Canada, that number remains less than 5%. But whatever you choose, the advice channel or direct, the construction of the investment portfolio remains the most critical element of the investment process, and higher costs reduce performance.

Retirement Plans

My father talked about retiring, and buying an Airstream trailer and traveling across the country, but my mother had no intentions of going anywhere in a trailer, and they never did. In fact, my father worked until the day he died. My neighbors talked about winterizing their cottage and retiring to Pickle Lake. Although they eventually winterized the cottage, they bought a townhouse in Toronto and didn't retire to Pickle Lake. My other neighbor retired for a short time but is now back working. Other friends wanted to retire and run a bed-and-breakfast. When she retired, and he semiretired, they actually did open a bed-and-breakfast. My point here is while small and unscientific, this sample statistically shows that only 33% of retirees actually fulfilled their plans of retirement, and 100% are working in retirement. The point is that all this financial planning, saving and investing should be within the context of people's lives.

The first Airstream trailer, "The Clipper," was built in 1936 and sold for $1,200. Today, more than 100,000 Airstream trailers have been built and about 60% still survive.

Although financial planning is a large component of retirement planning, don't overlook the social element to retirement that no amount of number crunching can replace. With 62% of Canadians planning to work during retirement, clearly you and your partner need to discuss your future plans to work.

My father worked until he died at age 82. For him and most others, the value of work goes far beyond financial need—it is also intrinsically linked to self-esteem, personal worth, companionship, boredom and purpose of being. Be aware that the concept of complete cessation of work for someone who has worked consistently for the past 40 years carries with it not simply financial implications, but also social and psychological ones. Statistics show that most people do not intend to stop work completely when they retire. Instead, they usually plan to work at what they want, when they want. In fact, many people plan completely new careers as a retirement goal.

Conclusions

You now understand how much money you might really need in order to retire, and you are aware of the limits of the social net in Canada and at what level you need to exceed that amount to make your investment efforts worthwhile. If you are a woman, you also understand the potential added financial requirements you face. You are also aware of why probability is a better way to understand the outcome of your investments than risk. You now know how to do a future value calculation and where to go to get or use these calculators, and you've discussed retirement with your spouse so you have a shared understanding.

You also understand that there is market risk. There is risk to capital. There is management risk and the risk of volatility. But the greatest risk, and the least understood risk, is the risk you unknowingly create, and that's the risk of outliving your money. Remember, at the end of the day, it's all in your hands.

"Every man is the architect of his own fortune."
Appius Claudius

2 "So You Think You Know about Investing?"

I am always surprised how little knowledge is transferable from one area of expertise to another. For instance, all the medical or accounting expertise in the world doesn't prepare you to be a good investor. If anything, such experiences can leave you with values and judgments that ill prepare you for the world of investing.

> "Knowledge born of actual experience is the answer to why one profits: lack of it is the reason one loses."
>
> *Gerald M. Loeb*

Think back to the early 1980s. The benchmark Canadian bond at the time, the 9 1/2 01s (9.5% annual dividend maturing in the year 2001), was trading at about 55 cents on the dollar and eventually traded close to 50 cents. One of my clients was an economist, a Ph.D., and he believed that he knew where interest rates were going, not only from day to day but hour to hour, so he wanted to trade bonds. My job is execution, not advice. It's similar to being the driver in the Monte Carlo Rally, where the navigator gets to make all the critical decisions about where to turn or how fast to go, but you're responsible for the consequences.

The economist showed up on the heels of a board presentation I had just made to a large Ottawa institutional client, whose investment portfolio was loaded with bonds. The portfolio was down $22 million, representing a loss of more than 40%. They wanted to sell out and take their losses because they thought we were going the way of Brazil and workers needed to be paid daily because inflation will drive up the price of bread by suppertime. But I just couldn't get my head around the Canada-equals-Brazil theme, probably because it's Ottawa, it's 20 below zero and we'd been skating on the canal now for eight weeks.

They had lots of cash accumulation because they'd been like deer, frozen in the headlights of the car for the past few years as the bond market moved against them. So I advised them to double up their position and buy another $22 million; I didn't even dare figure out my commission. They thought I was crazy and they couldn't bring themselves to buy anything, let alone another $22 million of bonds. I must have scared them about the possibility of a market reversal because they decided not to sell. The meeting was within months of the beginning of the greatest bond rally in Canadian history—a rally that lasted 17 years. If they had sold, they would have cemented a $22-million loss from which there would have been no recovery.

Despite the fact that bonds, unlike stocks, usually all go up or down together, my trader can't get on the right side of the market and the capital in the account is dwindling. I deliberately use the word trader instead of investor because my client never held a position for more than a few days. In the bond market, it's common for traders to go long; that is, to buy bonds and sell them later at a higher price, or go short, sell them without owning them, hoping to buy them later at a lower price. This allows an inexperienced trader the opportunity to lose money, regardless of which way interest rates go.

In the background, Dr. Doom and Dr. Gloom, Paul Volcker, former chairman of the Federal Reserve Board, and Henry Kaufman, economist with Salomon Brothers, are periodically giving little luncheon talks that move interest rates in the most unexpected ways. Every bond trader in the free world wants to know why these guys can't eat at their desks.

Then one afternoon, after a particularly unrewarding set of bond trades, my trader has one of those tragically flawed conclusions born of frustration and desperation.

"I've got it figured out. We'll open two parallel accounts. In one, we'll short $100,000 bonds and in the other, we'll go long $100,000," he explains with a tone of why-didn't-I-think-of-this-sooner.

"Then once the bonds start to move, we'll close out the losing account and ride the winner to glory."

I'm sure every seasoned compliance officer in the brokerage industry has a name for this, but all I can think of is he's lost it and how am I going to break it to him.

It's at that very moment that I realized that no amount of schooling or unrelated experience fully prepares you for the day when your own hard-earned money is at risk—you're up there without a net and the only thing between you and a margin call is your own wits.

> "Selling a soybean contract short is worth two years at the Harvard School of Business."
>
> *Robert Stovall*

In the early 1980s, McLeod Young and Weir did a deal with Shearson, the big U.S. brokerage, and part of the deal was that we got their Canadian commodities operation. So all the McLeod brokers, myself included, became licensed to trade commodities. Being a big believer in experience, I opened my own commodities account and deposited $10,000. It didn't take long before I had lost it all, but I was disciplined and that was my limit for the year. For the next five years, I started with $10,000 in early January. In the five years, the furthest I made it was to October before I lost the $10,000. Although I know a great deal about trading commodities, I still don't know enough or have the ability to apply the knowledge to profit from it.

Test Your Knowledge

Take the following quiz to see where you stand as to general market knowledge. One hundred fifty-seven points are up for grabs. There are no multiple choices in real life and there aren't any here either. Good luck.

Q. What is the Rule of 72?

A. If you divide 72 by the annualized rate of return, you'll find the number of years required for your capital to double, i.e., a 7.2% return divided into 72 takes 10 years to double your capital. It's a quick mental tool to check how well you have done or where you should be in a certain number of years. **2 pts.**

Q. Define real rates of return. Why are they important? And what are historic real rates of return?

A. Real rates of return are returns after inflation and they are important because they reflect the purchasing power of money. In recent years, with inflation in the 2% to 3% range and rates of return in the 15% to 25% range, real rates of return are well in excess of 10%. Before the 1980s, historic levels were 3% to 4% at best. When you are considering your retirement needs, take what you need to live on today and use an inflation adjustment to calculate your retirement needs. The Opus 2 Direct retirement calculator has just such an inflation adjustment built into it that you can turn on or off to see the effect of inflation on your retirement needs. **3 pts.** www.opus2direct.com/planner3.html

Q. What is the difference between book value and market value, and why is it important in your RRSP?

A. Book value is what you paid for the security and market value is what it is trading at, at any given moment in the market. This is important in your RRSP because now 25% foreign-content limits are determined using book value, not market value. Capital gain/loss is the difference between book and market value. **3 pts.**

Q. Two brothers start on an investment journey with $100,000. Brother A invests his money in a properly diversified portfolio and receives an 8% return in the first year and has $108,000. Brother B chases the hot funds and ends up investing in a fund just as the performance is coming off and loses 8% in the first year, leaving him with $92,000. Brother A continues on his portfolio strategy and again receives a modest 8% return and finishes the second year with $116,640.

- **What rate of return does Brother B need in Year Two to catch up with Brother A by year-end?**
- **What are the two most important things to consider in performance?**
  - **Near-past historic rates of return (hot funds)?**
  - **Probability of returns?**
  - **Capital protection?**

A. Brother B needs 26.78% in the second year just to pull even with Brother A. There are no asset classes that present a high probability of returns at those levels, so Brother B could be moved to desperate acts, which, from a probability standpoint, are likely to end in disaster. Capital protection and probability of returns are the most important factors. Scientific evidence has shown that chasing hot funds is a proven prescription for loss of capital and lower returns. **4 pts.**

$24,640 The 26.78% Difference

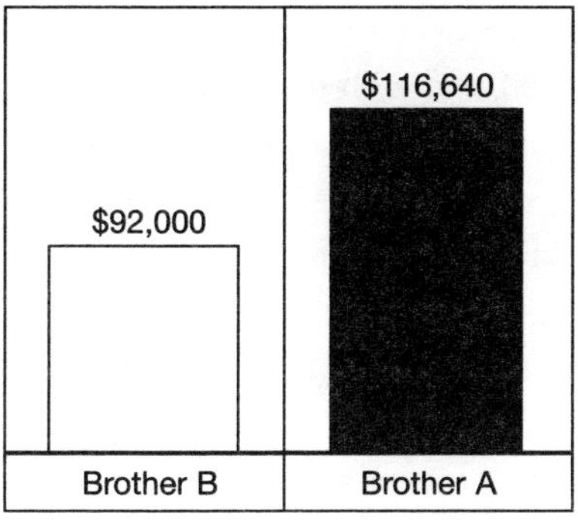

Q. A wise 25-year-old sets out on a quest to become wealthy beyond the comprehension of her peers, armed only with patience and a moderate 9% yield professionally constructed portfolio, aided by compounding without taxation. She opens an RRSP at age 25 in which she contributes $13,500 each year until retirement at age 60. How much money awaits our investor? A guess within $500,000 either way will suffice.

A. A total of $3,187,683 awaits the investor. Compounding is a beautiful thing. **2 pts.**

Q. Women are breaking through the glass ceiling. Who was the first female CEO of a Fortune 500 Company and a Dow stock, and what was the name of the company? Name the first female director and president of GM Canada. Name Canada's first female vice chairman of a Canadian bank.

A. Carly Fiorina, CEO of Hewlett Packard; Maureen Kempston Darkes, director and president of GM Canada; and Suzanne LaBarge, vice chairman of the Royal Bank. **3 pts.**

Q. At the turn of the century there were only three women CEOs in the Fortune 500 Companies. Besides Carly Fiorina, can you name the other two?

A. Marion O. Sandler, CEO of Golden West Financial Corp., and Andrea Jung, CEO of Avon. **2 pts.**

Q. The World Wide Web is an important part of today's investment world. What do you know about its inventor?

A. Tim Berners-Lee invented the web in 1989, wrote the first web client browser and server in 1990, and is presently the 3COM Founders Chair at the laboratory for computer sciences at MIT. **2 pts.**

Q. What is the incredible January barometer?

A. January's performance predicts the performance for the upcoming year, and since 1950, in 44 of the past 49 years, if January is up, then so will the S&P, or vice versa. In 2000, it opened at 11,357 on January 3 and was down to 10,940 on

January 31, so the odds are greater than 90% that 2000 will be a down year. **2 pts.**

Q. What is a price/earnings (P/E) ratio, and what is an average P/E ratio for the TSE and an e-commerce company today?

A. It's simply the stock price of the company divided by its earnings per share. Because most e-commerce companies have no earnings, their P/E ratios are infinite. This explains why we won't find these companies in a value manager's portfolio. In early March, the TSE had a P/E ratio of about 40/1, but the historic average has been more in the 15/1 range. In recent years P/E ratios have not been as widely used, as attention has shifted to cash flow for analysis. **5 pts.**

P/E Ratio Dow and TSE 300: 1990 to 2000

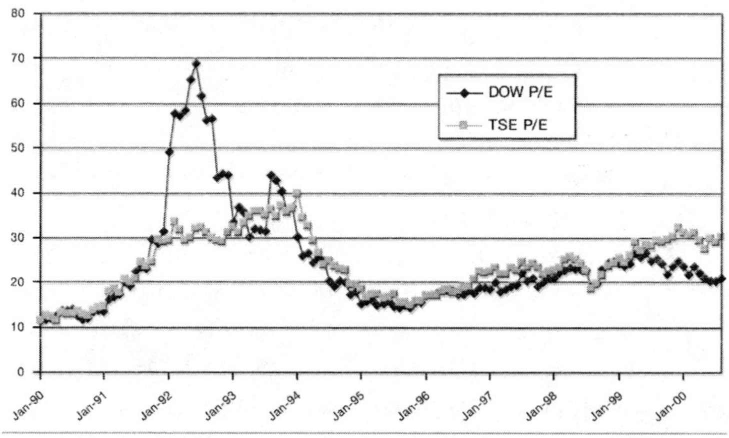

Q. Who were Dow and Jones and what were they famous for?

A. Charles Dow and Edward D. Jones began printing the Dow Jones news sheet in 1883, which detailed daily financial news. This publication was the precursor to *The Wall Street Journal,* which was first published on July 8, 1889, and of which Dow became an editor. **2 pts.**

Q. What is GARP?

A. A style of managing money defined as "growth at a reasonable price." This is fundamentally a growth-management philosophy with a value due-diligence process applied to the price of the stock at the time of purchase. **2 pts.**

Q. What is a momentum manager?

A. A growth manager who buys stocks without regard for price. He or she buys into the stock as the price trends upward and sells as the momentum wanes. Early 2000 turned out to be a tough period for momentum players, with record 700-point intraday moves on April 14, 2000. **3 pts.**

Q. Who are Graham and Dodds, and why are they important?

A. They are the fathers of value investing. Their work, *Security Analysis* published in 1934, is the basis of modern value investing. Their approach is based on the belief that purchasing stocks with lower price-earnings ratios generates higher returns over the long term. **2 pts.**

Q. Define the term margin and explain why there are concerns about its use today.

A. Margin is the use of borrowed money within a brokerage account to buy securities. A trader can usually only borrow up to 50% of the market value of the security. If the security drops in value, the trader must add cash to "cover the margin call." If he or she is unable to do so, sufficient securities are sold to bring the account "back on side" within the 50% margin requirement. At the end of March 2000, $278.5 billion were in margin in the United States and at the end of May that number was down to $240.7 billion. There have been recent concerns that if there was a serious market correction, this record level of margin could precipitate widespread margin-call selling, resulting in a disastrous correction. **3 pts.**

Q. What is relative price-to-sales ratio?

A. The ratio of stock price to sales per share. In recent years some value managers have moved to include this measure along with, or in lieu of, P/E evaluation because they feel price per sale gets closer to analyzing cash flow, which is less subject to distortion than earnings and thus gives a better view of the true value of a company. Their main concern is that distortion of earnings and the variation between companies as to how earnings are reported have changed the nature of P/E from the measurement that it once was. **2 pts.**

Price/Sales for Hewlett Packard 1987 to 2000,
The price rose from $10 to over $120

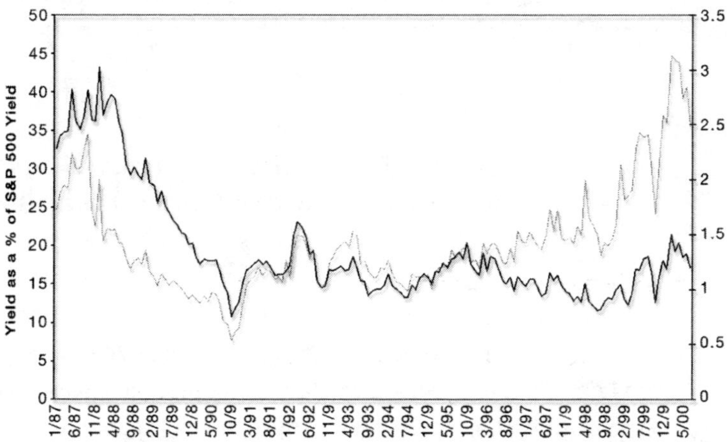

Q. Has the market of recent years favored a growth or value management style?

A. It's been growth all the way. Stocks with no earnings on the NASDAQ exchange in December 1999 were up an average of 50%, while stocks with earnings were down 2%. However, prior to recent years, value investing has always outperformed growth. In fact, in the United States, the Russell 200 Value Index beat the Russell Growth Index by 480 basis points, based on average annual compound returns from 1979–97. Early 2000 showed that there is life yet in value investing, but over the last year ending June 30, 2000, the Russell Growth was up 97.7% while the Russell Value could only manage 8% returns. **2 pts.**

Russell Growth & Value
10/1992–2000

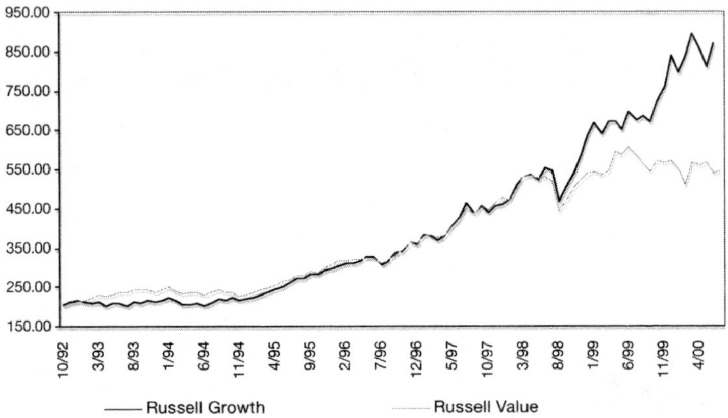

Q. Keeping in mind the earlier question about margin, what was the Tulip Mania and why is it food for thought in today's market?

A. The Tulip Mania is considered the most famous example of untrammeled speculation. It is hard to imagine, but in the 1600s tulip bulbs were a commodity that was traded like gold or silver. Tulip bulbs were bought and sold and traded like stock in hopes that the demand would increase and the price would rise. Such trading became widespread, much like recent-day Internet stocks and day trading. In 1636–37, this speculation and gambling, involving the price of bulbs of tulips and hyacinths, reached the point where a single bulb traded for thousands of guilders. This was at a time when the annual salary of the mayor of the district of Haarlem, the actual center of speculation, was only 500 guilders. But in 1637, with no warning, prices collapsed. Not only were fortunes lost and people thrown into ruin, but the Dutch monetary system was also threatened. Since the Dutch were significant players in world commerce, the collapse also caused problems in London, Paris and the rest of Europe. **3 pts.**

Q. So, while we are on the subject of disasters, explain what you know about the South Sea Bubble.

A. In 1711, the British government was in debt to the tune of £10 million, and the South Sea Trading Company, a group of merchants, then bought £9 million of the debt for a 6% return. To finance the purchase until other investments in the New World and the interest payments started, the company issued shares of the South Sea Trading Company. The whole scheme was based on the wealth of the New World, in particular South American gold to finance the debt purchases. In fact, in 1719, the Bank of England sold another £31 million of debt to anxious investors. Returns from the New World never materialized and in one day in September 1720, there were no more buyers. In fact, there were no buyers at all. Prices collapsed, and companies and families in both the New and Old Worlds were thrown into ruin. **3 pts.**

If you're fascinated by such events, you must read *Extraordinary Popular Delusions & the Madness of Crowds,* written by Charles MacKay in 1841.

> "What's my return on investment (ROI) on e-commerce?
> Are you crazy, this is Columbus in the New World.
> What was his ROI?"
>
> *Andy Grove*

Q. Who is undoubtedly the most famous value manager of all time and what is the name of his publicly traded company?

A. Warren Buffett of Omaha, Nebraska, and the company is Berkshire Hathaway, which traded at a 52-week high of $81,100 about a year ago. Recently it traded as low as $41,000. The recent market has not been kind to value managers, even the best of them. Warren Buffett's annual reports are a must-read for every value investor. **2 pts.**
www.berkshirehathaway.com/annual.html

Q. What is Warren Buffett's beef with stock options?

A. He strongly believes they are not properly accounted for by accounting and audit firms. Thus, they represent hidden compensation costs as well as outstanding shares that are not counted in share evaluations and, therefore, corporations with big option plans overstate their share values and understate their compensation costs. **2 pts.**

Q. The Toronto Stock Exchange has 35 stocks in its bellwether TSE 35 index. Can you name five of these stocks?

A. Abitibi Consolidated Inc., Alcan Aluminium Ltd., Bank of Montreal, Bank of Nova Scotia, Barrick Gold Corporation, BCE Inc., Biochem Pharma Inc., Bombardier Inc., Canadian Imperial Bank of Commerce, Canadian National Railway, Canadian Occidental Petroleum Ltd., Canadian Pacific Ltd., Canadian Tire Corp., Celestica Inc., Dofasco Inc., Inco Limited, Laidlaw Inc., Magna International Inc., Moore Corporation Ltd., National Bank of Canada, Noranda Inc., Nortel Networks Corporation, Nova Chemicals Corporation, Petro-Canada, Placer Dome Inc., Renaissance Energy Ltd., Royal Bank of Canada, Seagram Company Ltd., Suncor Energy Inc., Talisman Energy Inc., Teck Corp., Thomson Corporation, Toronto-Dominion Bank, Transalta Corporation and TransCanada Pipelines Ltd. **5 pts.**

Q. Only one stock has remained in the Dow from the beginning. What is it?

A. General Electric (GE). **2 pts.**

Q. Who is the CEO of General Electric and what is he famous for?

A. The CEO is Jack Welsh, considered by many to be the best manager in corporate America and credited with the wholesale restructuring and success of GE. **3 pts.** www.ge.com

"If you're looking up at me (the boss), you've got your ass pointed at the customer."

Jack Welsh

Q. What is EBITDA?

A. A financial analysis term used to indicate cash flow after costs, but specifically refers to "earnings before interest, taxes, depreciation and amortization." This number provides the analyst with a feel for the real usable cash generation of a company, and as cash-flow analysis becomes more and more important, so does EBITDA. **4 pts.**

Q. What is burn rate, and why is it important for so many dot.com companies?

A. Burn rate is the amount of cash that a company goes through on a monthly basis, when its revenue is below its costs (this is usually the case for most dot.com start-ups). The problem is that most dot.com companies have a finite amount of capital and their burn rate may be such that they burn up their supply of capital before they can reach breakeven and produce a profit, resulting in the need to raise further capital or declare bankruptcy. **3 pts.**

Q. Name the site of North America's first oil well and the date on which and depth to which it was drilled.

A. In 1845 or 1855, Charles Tripp dug only two meters or six feet in Oil Springs, Ontario, Canada, located 35 kilometers south of Sarnia, and hit oil when he was actually looking for water. Tripp never appreciated the find and sold it to James Miller, who extracted over 1.5 million liters of oil from 1858–60, beating American Edwin L. Drake of Titusville, Pennsylvania, by three years, who is often mistakenly credited with North America's first oil well. **2 pts.**

Q. What is the size of a futures lumber contract and why?

A. 110,000 board feet, because it is the amount of lumber that fits on a standard 57 1/2-foot railway car. **2 pts.**

Q. The Dow Jones Industrial Average was started with 12 companies on May 26, 1896, priced at 40.94. Can you name any of the original 12 Dow companies?

A. American Cotton Oil, American Sugar, American Tobacco, Chicago Gas, Distilling and Cattle Feeding, General Electric, Laclede Gas, National Lead, North American, Tennessee Coal & Iron, U.S. Leather Preferred and U.S. Rubber. **2 pts.**

Q. At one time, there was a Canadian company in the Dow. It was removed during the 1990s. Can you name it?

A. Inco International Nickel Company. **2 pts.**

Q. If a company is totally connected to a community, its name is often the same as the city in which it is located; for example, Hershey Chocolate of Hershey, Pennsylvania. Can you name three other such communities?

A. Corning, New York, Corning Glass,
Corbyville, Ontario, Corby's Distilleries,
Batawa, Ontario, Bata Shoes and
Oshkosh, Wisconsin, Oshkosh Jeans. **3 pts.**

Q. Today, there are 30 Dow stocks. Can you name five of these stocks?

A. Alcoa, American Express, AT&T, Boeing, Caterpillar, Citigroup, Coca-Cola, Dupont, Eastman Kodak, Exxon, General Electric, General Motors, Home Depot, Honeywell International, Hewlett Packard, IBM, Intel, International Paper, J. P. Morgan, Johnson & Johnson, McDonald's, Merck, Microsoft, 3M, Philip Morris, Procter & Gamble, SBC Communications, United Technologies, Wal-Mart Stores and Walt Disney. **5 pts.**

Q. When was the last time the Canadian dollar traded at par and who was the prime minister?

A. The year was 1976 and Pierre Elliott Trudeau was prime minister. **2 pts.**

Q. Which minister of finance for which government brought in the capital gains tax and when?

A. The minister of finance was Edgar J. Benson and the prime minister was Pierre Elliott Trudeau. The year was 1972. **3 pts.**

Q. Two of the most powerful men in Canada and the United States are Canada's Governor of the Bank of Canada and the United States Chairman of the Federal Reserve Board. Who were the last three people to hold these posts?

A. Bank of Canada Governors: Gordon Thiessen, 1994–present; John Crow, 1987–94; and Gerald Bouey, 1973–87. Federal Reserve Bank Chairmen: Alan Greenspan, 1987–present; Paul Volcker, 1979–87; G. William Miller, 1978–79. **6 pts.**

Q. What does Chapter 11 refer to and what is the Canadian equivalent?

A. Chapter 11 is a U.S. law that allows a company to continue to operate while in bankruptcy rather than be liquidated. The Canadian equivalent is the Canada Creditor Protection Act. **2 pts.**

Q. What was the highest rate paid on Canada Savings Bonds, in which year and what was the prime rate?

A. The year was 1981; the CSB rate was 19.5%; and the prime rate was 17.25%. The central bank rate at the time the bonds were issued was 15.4%. **3 pts.**

Q. Name the Canadian-born economist who recently won the Nobel Prize for Economics. What was his idea?

A. Robert A. Mundell won the Nobel Prize for his analysis of monetary and fiscal policy under different exchange rate regimes and his analysis of optimum currency areas. His work suggests that a strong currency is the cornerstone of economic growth and was the fundamental basis for the new Euro and U.S. policies under President Ronald Reagan that produced a strong currency and fueled the greatest growth period in U.S. history. His views were the antithesis of those of Kenneth Galbraith, perhaps Canada's best-known economist. **3 pts.**

As an aside: Alfred Nobel amassed a fortune, principally from his invention of dynamite in 1866. Believed to be influenced by Bernard

Shaw's work *Socialism for Millionaires* in 1894, which stated, "Never give the people everything they want. ... give them something they ought to want but don't," when Nobel died in 1896 he left behind a most remarkable will that bequeathed the bulk of his estate to the creation of the Nobel Prizes, the capital of which was to be invested in safe securities and the interest to be distributed annually in five equal parts to Nobel Prize recipients. Although Shaw himself actually won the prize for literature in 1925, he refused the money.

Q. What is placer gold, and what role did it play in the Bre-X scandal? When was the Yukon Klondike gold rush?

A. Placer gold is gold that washes free and is found in streambeds. The action of tumbling along in the gravel makes the tiny gold nuggets rounded, unlike their counterparts that are found imbedded in ore with telltale sharp-edge characteristics. In the Bre-X scandal, some early critics questioned the presence of gold with placer characteristics coming from supposed ore samples; they were right. Gold was first discovered in the Yukon in 1878, but the real Canadian Klondike gold rush was at its peak from 1897–98. **3 pts.**

Q. What famous Canadian poet wrote about the Canadian gold rush? Quote at least two lines from the poem.

A. Robert Service, "The Cremation of Sam McGee."
"There are strange things done in the midnight sun
By the men who moil for gold;
The Arctic trails have their secret tales
That would make your blood run cold;
The Northern Lights have seen queer sights,
But the queerest they ever did see
Was that night on the marge of lake Lebarge
I cremated Sam McGee."
Moil—what a great word; it means drudgery as in toil and moil, a perfect word to describe what life in the gold fields of the late 1800s must have been like. **3 pts.**

Q. In 1979–80, two well-known investors tried to corner the silver market. Who were they and what price did silver rise to?

A. In 1979, Warren Buffett of Berkshire Hathaway bought more than 125 million ounces of silver, which was curious because silver doesn't meet any of the traditional values expounded by Buffett; however, Berkshire had cash and inflation was raging. Next, the Hunt brothers, Nelson and Herbert, used borrowed money to buy silver and the price went from less than $10 in 1979 to more than $50 in 1980. At this point Buffett decided to get out. Then the United States Federales changed the margin rules on silver. The Hunts got a multibillion-dollar margin call, couldn't make it and were forced to sell. Silver dropped back to less than $10 and has never recovered. **3 pts.**

Silver Prices U.S. per ounce London Fix

Year	High	Low	Average
1999	5.4811	5.0315	5.2182
1998	7.8100	4.6900	5.5442
1997	6.2675	4.2235	4.8972
1996	5.8275	4.7100	5.1995
1995	6.0375	4.4160	5.1971
1994	5.7475	4.6400	5.2851
1993	5.4200	3.5600	4.3130
1992	4.3350	3.6475	3.9464
1991	4.5710	3.5475	4.0566
1990	5.3560	3.9500	4.8316
1989	6.2100	5.0450	5.4999
1988	7.8215	6.0500	6.5324
1987	10.9250	5.3600	7.0156
1986	6.3100	4.8530	5.4645
1985	6.7500	5.4500	6.1319
1984	10.1100	6.2200	8.1446
1983	14.6680	8.3700	11.4301
1982	11.1100	4.9010	7.9219
1981	16.3030	8.0300	10.4869
1980	49.4500	10.8900	20.9837
1979	32.2000	5.9350	11.0679
1978	6.2640	4.8180	5.4218
1977	4.9750	4.3130	4.6333
1976	5.0840	3.8300	4.3532
1975	5.2110	3.9280	4.4256

www.silverinstitute.org

"Every crowd has a silver lining."
P. T. Barnum

Q. What is the annualized rate of return for the TSE for the past five and 10 years?

A. It will no doubt come as a surprise to many, but Canadian markets have been outstanding performers over the past five and 10 years. Admittedly, returns have been skewed in recent years, but average annual compound returns for the TSE 300 were 16.98% for five years and 10.55% for 10 years, and in the last year were up a remarkable 31.71% ending December 31, 1999. **2 pts.**

Q. Which company accounts for the largest percentage weighting of the TSE and how much is that weighting? Name the company's CEO.

A. After the BCE spin-off of Nortel in April 2000, it alone accounted for 32.3% of the TSE 300 and BCE 2.3%. Nortel's CEO is John Roth. If you're even close, give yourself 3 points. The TSE 300 is now so overweighted by Nortel/BCE that professional managers are beginning to refer to the TSE 298 (minus BCE and Nortel) or, after the split, the TSE 299 (minus Nortel), believing that this reflects better the performance of the Canadian market. **5 pts.**

TSE 300/298 1-year returns ending June 30, 2000

TSE 300 47.4%
Nortel accounts for 21.7%
Bell accounts for 9.3%

TSE 298 returns (minus Nortel/BCE) 16.4%

Q. What is the annualized rate of return for the Dow for the past five and 10 years?

A. Average annual compound rates of return for the Dow Jones Industrial Average for the same five- and 10-year periods were 24.56% and 15.37% respectively, ending December 31, 1999. **2 pts.**

Q. One index continues to outperform the Dow Jones Industrial Average. What is it and what does it stand for? How many companies are represented in it?

A. This index is the NASDAQ, which comprises 5,800+ issues. For the past 10 years, it rose 794% versus 317% on the Dow; five years, 441% for NASDAQ versus 199% for the Dow; 85.58% last year versus 25.22% for the Dow, ending December 31, 1999. However, this has not been the case in 2000, which may be the first year in some time in which the Dow outperforms the NASDAQ. NASDAQ is an acronym for National Association of Securities Dealers Automated Quotation and it first traded on February 8, 1971. **3 pts.**

Q. What is the MSCI and what is it best known for? What role does Canada play in the MSCI?

A. MSCI stands for the Morgan Stanley Capital International. It is best known for a family of indices that reflect various world markets and its premier benchmark is the world index. The December 31, 1999, regional weightings were 49% U.S., 13.4% Japan, 9.4% U.K., 5.1% Germany, 5% France, 2.8% Switzerland, 2.6% Netherlands and 2.1% Canada. It was up 25.34% last year, 20.25% over five years and 11.96% on a 10-year basis. **3 pts.**

Q. What is the EAFE and what were its five- and 10-year returns?

A. EAFE stands for Europe, Australasia, Far East. This index tracks returns in these areas. Average annual compound rates of return for these periods were 13.15% for the most recent five years and 7.34% for the most recent 10 years, ending December 31, 1999, and a respectable 27.30% last year. **3 pts.**

Market Returns Ending December 31, 1999

December 1999	Stock Price Index Value	Total Return Index Value	1-Year Total Return	3-Year Total Return	5-Year Total Return	10-Year Total Return	15-Year Total Return
TSE 300 Composite	8,413.75	17,977.46	31.71	14.23	16.98	10.55	11.77
METALS & MINERALS	4,474.82	8,354.15	48.40	-3.42	3.28	5.51	8.58
GOLD & PRECIOUS MINERALS	4,875.33	7,092.41	-16.99	-23.88	-12.03	-3.00	4.39
OIL & GAS	5,861.73	7,877.62	27.26	-2.58	8.23	4.04	6.20
PAPER & FOREST PRODUCTS	5,236.84	10,999.99	49.52	5.89	4.76	5.27	8.98
CONSUMER PRODUCTS	15,436.00	36,034.34	28.74	18.77	20.92	13.48	13.76
INDUSTRIAL PRODUCTS	9,789.29	19,402.54	103.75	36.74	30.07	19.43	14.73
REAL ESTATE	2,013.47	3,051.11	-14.98	-3.96	0.34	-17.06	-6.07
TRANSPORTATION & ENVIRON	5,283.51	8,180.35	-12.51	-4.31	2.87	-5.41	4.32
PIPELINES	4,206.93	14,184.81	-30.00	-0.14	7.41	7.15	9.79
UTILITIES	12,563.86	45,797.56	73.23	44.15	34.65	20.44	17.46
COMMUNICATIONS & MEDIA	16,274.15	31,990.07	7.84	18.65	16.40	9.25	12.58
MERCHANDISING	5,114.78	10,693.90	-8.82	3.42	8.97	3.06	8.33
FINANCIAL SERVICES	7,410.36	24,231.28	-9.80	13.25	22.18	14.06	14.65
CONGLOMERATES	8,723.76	20,470.83	7.95	6.29	14.84	7.11	10.40
Toronto 35	480.16	852.19	38.98	17.35	19.24	11.58	12.52
SM 91 Day T-Bills		275.97	4.66	4.20	4.99	6.59	7.68
SM Bond Universe		386.33	-1.14	5.77	9.90	10.09	10.84
DJIA in US$	11,497.12		25.22	21.26	24.56	15.37	16.19
DJIA in C$	16,592.76		18.08	23.39	25.29	17.93	16.87
NASDAQ in US$	4,069.31		85.58	46.62	40.17	24.50	20.53
NASDAQ in C$	5,872.87		75.00	49.20	40.99	27.27	21.24
S&P 500 in US$	1,469.25	2,021.40	21.04	27.56	28.56	18.21	18.94
S&P 500 in C$	2,120.44	2,917.31	14.14	29.80	29.31	20.84	19.64
MS EAFE in US$	1,760.04	4,128.81	27.30	16.06	13.15	7.34	16.29
MS EAFE in C$	2,540.11	5,958.74	20.04	18.10	13.81	9.72	16.98
MS WORLD in US$	1,420.89	3,731.56	25.34	22.05	20.25	11.96	17.07
MS WORLD in C$	2,050.64	5,385.42	18.20	24.19	20.95	14.45	17.75
MS EUROPE 15 in C$	2,202.01	6,934.47	9.60	25.16	23.26	17.04	20.87
MS JAPAN in C$	5,153.79	8,303.72	52.55	11.11	2.72	1.52	12.39
MS PACIFIC ex JAPAN in C$		3,077.89	35.03	-0.68	5.60	12.47	14.67
MS WORLD ex USA in C$		5,835.03	20.96	18.19	14.09	9.82	16.56
MS EMF Latin Am. C$	1,619.13		46.61	9.21	5.15	18.65	-

Q. What is a mutual fund MER and why does it not tell the full story?

A. MER stands for management expense ratio (MER) and it is the amount taken from the fund annually, usually expressed to consumers as a percentage, such as 2.40%. Within the industry, however, these fees are typically referred to in basis points—1/100th of a percent. Thus, an MER of 2.40% would be referred to as 240 beeps. The MER includes profit to the manufacturer, commission to the salesperson, money management costs, legal costs, filling costs, accounting costs and others. It does not, however, reflect all fees as in the case of WRAP products, or performance fees, or front-end loads or back-end loads, account or RRSP fees, or asset-allocation fees, which, when applicable, are in addition to the annual MER. **3 pts.**

Q. What is the average price paid for an equity mutual fund in Canada?

A. The average price paid is 235 basis points or 2.35%, but this does not reflect front- or back-end loads. Today, most funds are sold using back-end or deferred sales charges that occur only if and when the investor sells the funds, usually within a seven-year period. However, the average investor seldom holds the fund investments that long and data show that the holding period is decreasing from an average of eight to nine years to fewer than three years today. So, if the average investor holds a mutual fund for five years, he or she would trigger an additional 250 basis points, or 2.5% or more, of deferred sale charges. However, this still doesn't take into account any fees such as asset allocation, account opening, performance or RRSP fees that might be charged. This brings the annual gross cost of a Canadian equity mutual fund held for an average of five years to just under 300 basis points or 3%. This amount is a conservative estimate of what the average Canadian investor actually pays annually to own an equity mutual fund in Canada. For further information, refer to the *National Post* or *Globe and Mail.* Both newspapers publish MERs and any additional fees that are applicable to the specific fund investment in their monthly *Mutual Fund Report.* **4 pts.**

Q. Why do mutual funds in the United States seem cheaper?

A. It is generally accepted that in Canada the cost of funds is higher, but this cost may not be as great as it first seems. First, more than 40% of U.S. funds, as opposed to less than 5% of Canadian funds, are distributed direct—with the inherently lower fee structure. Second, Canadian MERs include some, but not all, sales commissions. In the United States, sales commissions are not included in the MERs; they are stated separately in what is known as the 12B1 fee, making our MERs larger. Finally, when averages are used, Americans do not invest as much on a percentage basis in the more expensive foreign equities and they have higher percentages in the lower-cost fixed-income funds, in particular, nontaxable municipal bond funds. **3 pts.**

Q. The issue of what Canadian mutual fund investors pay is extremely complicated. At a recent seminar, an attendee commented that he didn't pay any fees because he had a no-load fund. Many of the other attendees also thought this was the case. Then I asked them how a fund company could make a profit by selling funds with absolutely no fees. It then dawned on them that they had been misled. There is widespread misunderstanding by consumers about the costs of mutual funds. What has the Ontario Securities Commission (OSC) recently done to clarify the issue of mutual fund costs?

A. At the time of this writing, the Ontario Securities Commission, in response to this widespread confusion, has posted a mutual fund calculator to their web site that both explains and calculates the total costs of mutual funds to consumers. **2 pts.**

We recommend you go there even if you believe you know what you are paying. You may be surprised. www.osc.gov.on.ca/en/Investor/Tools/Mutual/ca01457e.html or you can try a simpler graphic site by Opus 2 Direct at www.opus2direct.com/calculators/MERCalculate.asp. Both the Opus 2 and OSC sites provide links to other calculators.

Q. Where does performance come from? What about the stock selection activity the manager is charged with? How about the asset-class selection that the portfolio designer is responsible for? Is the ability to move in and out of the market to enhance returns known as market timing, and the movement from one market to another known as tactical asset allocation?

A. Continual research by many different companies, including SEI, Morningstar, Frank Russell and Mercer, shows that more than 90% of all performance comes from the activity of portfolio design and asset-class selection. The activity of individual stock selection by professional money managers has marginal positive effect on performance of less than 10%. But a study by Dalbar in the United States showed that investors selecting and trading stocks on their own in a market that is generating 15%, actually suffered a severe negative effect of reducing performance by more than 60%; that is, to 6%. The same effect applies to market timing and tactical asset allocation. Various professional money managers specializing in tactical asset allocation have been able to add some positive value over time, but still less than 0.5%. Again, as the Morningstar study shows, individual trading in 219 growth funds over a five-year period, ending in May 1994, actually reduced the 12.5% performance of their investments by more than 80%; that is, to 2.2%. Research is overwhelming that the most important decision an investor makes is which asset classes he or she buys to build his or her portfolio and the most common mistakes are attempting to market-time and predict the hot funds or asset classes. **6 pts.**

Q. How did Wall Street get its name?

A. When New York was founded on February 2, 1653, it was then called New Amsterdam. The original Dutch settlers built a wall to protect themselves from Indian invasions on the tip of Manhattan Island. Wall Street today stands where the original wall was built almost 400 years ago. **2 pts.**

Q. Here's a question for all those budding economists out there. What is the difference between monetary policy and fiscal policy?

A. Monetary policy is the central bank's action to influence the availability and cost of money and credit, commonly referred to as money supply. Fiscal policy is related to taxation and public spending; a combination of both are used by governments to control economic growth, inflation and employment levels. **4 pts.**

Well, how did you do? A total of **157** points was up for grabs. I know the last question was a bit obtuse, but above 100 is good; if you scored below 100 you should seek professional financial help. Keep in mind we let you keep score yourselves so we assumed some leniency in the granting of points, so a solid 100 points or better was what we were looking for. Read on.

Before you begin thinking that being better informed can help you be a better investor, I'm here to tell you that it ain't necessarily so. Ironically, there's so much information out there today, what the media call clutter and noise, that most investors don't have a clear sense of what to do. That includes a proliferation of magazines, books, newspapers, TV programs and investment seminars, many of which didn't even exist a few years ago.

The Value of Information

You have to ask yourself what it is about information that makes it valuable to you. And yet information is only of value if you have it and others don't. But when everyone has it at the same time, to whom does it have value? This brings us to the ultimate challenge—how do we interpret the information? And can we achieve an advantage over other investors by more wisely or cleverly utilizing what has become commonplace?

I would argue that phenomena such as CNBC and the Internet have changed the value of financial information forever. These developments have made information so pervasive and instantaneous that they have actually made information valueless. But on the flip side, they have rejuvenated the value of experience and intellectual interpretation.

In a very real way, CNBC and the Internet have made what is old new again. By reducing the value of information, they have shifted the value away from information itself and instead towards the interpretation of that information, and placed renewed value on experience. Today, no investor can separate investing from the media—in particular, from the Internet.

Many investors attend seminars, hoping to be struck by a bolt of lightning, a nugget of insight that will illuminate their financial landscape. We're all looking for the Holy Grail—and finding confusion. The information playing field is now level. The information advantage that even a senior analyst at a major brokerage firm has over you, in your home study tuned to CNBC and wired into the web, is marginal. It is not surprising that arbitrary stock quote delays are maintained on web links to retain some semblance of advantage to those within the financial industry.

But before you proceed to the next chapter, in which we actually get closer to the Holy Grail of investing, here's some sage advice to remember dating back to the early 1700s.

"A little knowledge is a dangerous thing."
Alexander Pope

I wonder what Pope would have thought about the dangers of everyone having the information at the same time and what his advice might be today, keeping in mind that he was one of the clever people who profited from the South Sea Bubble by recognizing the situation early and shorting the stock.

No one decides to be their own doctor or dentist and remove their own appendix or perform their own root canal because we recognize that these are professions requiring years of training, and the consequences of an amateur effort are catastrophic. However, when it comes to investments we seem to ignore the same parameters that investing is a profession requiring years of training and that amateur efforts have serious negative effects.

Specialized Knowledge

Professional money management is a highly segmented business and most professionals in the field actually know a great deal about a very narrow range of the investment spectrum. For example, a bond trader may spend his professional life trading only short-duration Government of Canada bonds, while an equity trader may be focused only on Canadian large-capital value stocks or emerging markets. Although many of these skills are transferable, most professional money managers do not venture out of their narrow area of expertise. So, when you decide to construct a portfolio on your own by selecting asset classes and trading individual stocks, you are unknowingly assuming responsibility for a body of knowledge that would be embodied within a team of professional money managers with literally hundreds of years of combined experience.

The quiz presented earlier in this chapter would be easy for most professional money managers who have many years of training and experience behind them, yet they might still have trouble with the questions outside their area of expertise. This quiz should lead you to conclude that investing is not an amateur activity; to do well over a long period with your investments, you will need professional money and portfolio management.

Most wealthy people do not manage their own money. They seek professional advice to construct investment portfolios using professional money managers. I would argue that, in part, professional money management has contributed to their becoming and remaining wealthy. If you want to be wealthy, simply do what wealthy people do: get a properly designed investment portfolio managed by professional money managers.

3 "Some Assembly Required"

In this chapter we will discuss being an investor—not a trader but an investor. By definition this involves constructing a proper investment portfolio, not just an investment account that contains a series of unrelated mutual funds or stocks. The base from which all other investment activities must begin is an investment portfolio, and it should be every serious investor's first priority. An investment portfolio is the cornerstone to being an investor and the base from which a professional trader operates.

Have you ever wondered how you would manage your money if you had $100 million? Probably not. But now that you are thinking about it, do you think you would manage $100 million in the same way you presently manage your existing funds? Probably not. So, do you believe that people with large amounts of money manage their money differently—that is, professionally? Probably! And if you had that kind of money, would you be wise enough to find out how wealthy people manage their money and then use those same professionals and professional methods to manage yours? Probably. Do you think there is a correlation between managing money professionally and having large amounts of money? Probably. Do you believe that the corollary—that by managing small amounts of money professionally you can have larger amounts of money—is true? Probably. Then, is the only thing that stands between your present financial situation and that of being wealthier an understanding of how wealthy people professionally manage their money? Absolutely!

This truism—knowing how to manage money professionally—is all that stands between you and greater wealth. While very successful money management process is widely known, particularly within the high-net-worth, segregated and pension businesses, unfortunately it has been a well-kept secret from the general investing public. Why? Because this process is fee based, not transaction based, and therefore it generally reduces commission generation.

Think back to our earlier example of the two 30-year-old investors, each with $30,000, adding $10,000 to the investment per year, receiving a 10% return and then retiring at age 60. The trader risks the $30,000 and loses, then resumes saving and eventually retires with $1,644,939. The investor doesn't risk capital, just keeps investing and retires with $2,168,421. So, what seemed to be a simple $30,000 mistake at the beginning ultimately becomes a $523,482 error.

This is why it is paramount that you establish a portfolio early on, not a trading account. While capital protection is always important, it is most important at the beginning.

Learning from the Central Guaranty Trust

I learned these lessons concerning portfolio management through a somewhat circuitous route. In 1990, I was asked by a friend to leave Ottawa and move to Toronto to head up the trust department of Central Guaranty Trust as senior vice president of trust. The idea was to introduce a sales culture into the trust division in order to increase the fee-based assets under administration. I remember confiding in Edgar Benson, the former minister of finance who introduced capital gains into Canada in 1972 and also a family friend, as to whether I should change careers. His advice: "Every 10 years you should change careers just to stay fresh." And then he added, "For a politician, this is a justification for not being able to get reelected." Regardless, it seemed like good advice and I have always feared having one year's experience 40 times over as opposed to 40 years' experience.

"It is better to go through life as a student rather than a teacher, that way every day you learn something."
Raymond Moriyama

For me it is the adventure, not just the money. Over the years I have learned that people don't usually change jobs for money or for a new adventure. They move because of differences with management, principally personality conflicts. Thus it was for me. In Ottawa, I was no longer with McLeod Young and Weir. I am now with Dean Witter and my direct report was the manager from hell and while the Toronto move was a sizable reduction in income, it was one of the best decisions I have ever made.

Trust consisted of personal trust, pension trust and corporate trust, totaling just under $20 billion in assets—a considerable jump from the $40 million plus I was managing in Ottawa. And this was an epiphany for me and led to my greater understanding of how money should be managed. When you are responsible for managing lots of money, you're forced not only by, in this case, trust law, but also by fiduciary and moral obligation to manage it in a scientific and responsible manner. In the trust world, everything centers on capital protection to the exclusion of performance. Every action is measured against the "prudent man rule," which is essentially a reasonableness test. That is, before every financial action one must ask, "Would a prudent man act this way under these circumstances?" It's equivalent to an industry conscience, except that it is backed by the weight of law. In the trust industry, all accounts are discretionary and client consent is never an issue. You received client consent when the account was opened, and every transaction is measured by the prudent man rule.

The Brokerage Industry

The brokerage business, however, is very different from the trust industry in that it is principally driven by performance and trading transactions. Yet most brokerage firms have no way of assessing client account performance, although they have many ways of measuring the commission cash flow resulting from trading transactions. In the brokerage industry, every action is measured against client suitability, what used to be called KYC or "know your client" rules and client consent to every trade.

In the brokerage community, success is measured by commission generation; in the trust industry, by preservation of capital.

Imagine my position: an ex-broker, who had lived off commission, no salary, for the last 10 years, driven by performance in a pure sales environment, who was suddenly dropped into the trust industry, where I am surrounded by trust and trust investment offices obsessed with capital preservation. It was a tremendous experience, certainly the most intellectually influential experience I have had regarding managing people's money, and a day did not pass at Central Guaranty Trust that I didn't learn something.

"One man's ceiling is another man's floor."
Paul Simon

My experiences at Central Guaranty Trust taught me that people who have money behave quite differently from people who are trying to make money. People who are trying to make money often behave in ways that are not conducive to becoming a wealthy person. And, if by some fluke of luck they are successful in acquiring financial assets, they lack the skill sets to keep it.

My best advice about investing is a hybrid of the obsession with capital protection of the trust industry and the unyielding demands for performance of the brokerage industry.

So, when Central Guaranty Trust lost more than $600 million on its real estate holdings, the writing was on the wall, and I thought, who better than the brokerage industry to benefit from my new-found financial insights? Armed with a complete business plan to create a fee-based managed-money product with performance measurement, I approached Richardson Greenshields. They hired me on the basis of the business plan and we built Sovereign, Canada's first WRAP investment program.

The Beginning of WRAP Products in Canada

WRAP is based on a simple idea that all the services required to deliver the portfolio solution are wrapped up in one offering and at one fee. There are variations on this portfolio solution theme in the form of "funds to fund," which is a single mutual fund made up of other mutual funds, in such a combination as to represent a portfolio, and/or "asset-allocation programs" that model a portfolio using a wide choice of mutual funds, or as is more often the case, just the set of funds offered by the parent company. Although each option can be a good solution, you must watch the cost, particularly in the latter two where the layering of services can increase fees substantially. Some WRAP products and funds to fund can be expensive, so avoid them as they translate directly into lower performance.

This movement to portfolio-based managed product is the last of the skirmishes in what is the most important revolution in the retail financial industry. In recent years, there have been several great revolutions in the investment industry, but first and foremost is the battle surrounding how one should manage clients' money. There is now general agreement that the methodology known as "modern portfolio theory" is the accepted way to manage money and, for all practical purposes, this fight is now over. Individuals, corporations or pensions with large amounts of money will hire advisers such as William M. Mercer, Towers Perrin, SEI, Frank Russell or, in some cases, an individual, who will select the appropriate money managers to diversify by asset class and management style. On this point, there is general agreement within the industry; however, the message has yet to be conveyed to retail investors.

The story of "modern portfolio theory" began in 1990 when William Sharpe and Harry Markowitz won the Nobel Memorial Prize in Economic Science. Sharpe was responsible for his work on the capital asset pricing model that identifies which risk can be reduced by diversification and which risk cannot, and Markowitz was noted for his work on the efficient frontier that sets out the basis for trading off risk against returns. Today, most large pools of investment capital follow these proven scientific principles.

Financial planners have more readily accepted the idea of portfolio construction and asset allocation than have the brokers, who have been much slower to embrace the findings and methodologies of modern portfolio theory. As a result, clients have remained largely unaware of such options because it was not always in the best interest of these commission-driven industries to move to lower-payout, fee-based portfolio management products. In most cases, these fee-based portfolios have no initial commission payout.

> "In the future, brokers will be like
> small asset management companies."
> *Warren Buffett*

This situation is now changing, in many cases because institutions have corporate mandates to increase fee-based revenue and reduce the volatility of transaction-based revenue. In fact, many financial corporations are becoming more actively involved in the actual money management process and the construction of portfolio-based solutions. Many are promoting the virtues of modern portfolio theory through the introduction of corporately constructed retail products that embrace these principles. This is best seen in the proliferation of

WRAP programs, funds-to-fund portfolios and asset-allocation programs. Fortunately for consumers, many of the processes for the delivery of modern portfolio theory are fee-based.

The process of modern portfolio theory is a scientific recipe for investing. And as with any recipe, one must choose ingredients, which equates to the asset-class selection. And then one must ensure that the best quality of the ingredients is selected, which equates to the selection of money managers for the asset classes. And finally one must combine these ingredients in just the right way, which equates to the asset allocation.

The choice of asset-class selection and asset allocation is considered by most to have a far greater influence than manager selection. Until the investor realizes greater importance of asset-class selection and asset allocation, professional results cannot be achieved. Most investors overestimate the importance of the money manager in the investment process and are influenced by manager performance of the immediate past. This creates unrealistic expectations because they fail to realize the importance of the portfolio as a whole, and the importance of asset-class selection—with regrettable results.

For example, a high-quality Canadian manager (5-year TSE returns of 16.98%) would not outperform a mediocre U.S. manager (5-year S&P 500 returns of 28.56%) ending December 31, 1999. The choice of asset-class selection had a far greater influence than manager selection; if you still doubt this, look at the 20-year TSE 300 4.7-fold increase versus the Dow fourteenfold increase. There is no way that manager selection had a greater effect than asset-class selection over the last 20 years, and yet, retail investors and the popular press remain fixated on short-term manager performance.

The performance of the portfolio is the important issue, realizing that diversification does not come from holding many assets but from holding the right professionally selected assets that complement each other to enhance performance and reduce volatility.

TSE 300's 20-year 7.97% return/4.7-fold increase
Dow's 20-year 17.94% return/fourteen-fold increase
–ending December 31, 1999

The Efficient Frontier

This control of volatility and maximization of returns culminates in what is known as "the efficient frontier," which is simply a curved line representing an infinite set of portfolios that are considered to be efficient. That is, the combination of assets in the portfolio will deliver the lowest volatility for a portfolio of that yield or the highest yield for a portfolio of that volatility. It is for this idea that Markowitz won the Nobel Prize: that there are a set of investment portfolios that are fundamentally most efficient, in that for any given risk there is a way to maximize returns, or for any given rate of return there is a way to achieve it with minimum risk.

Most investors adopt a haphazard approach to portfolio construction, randomly adding various funds or stocks to an account over a period of time. This will most certainly result in an inefficient investment portfolio, one that has undue risk or one that has limits to its potential for returns.

7 Opus 2 Direct Portfolios on the Efficient Frontier

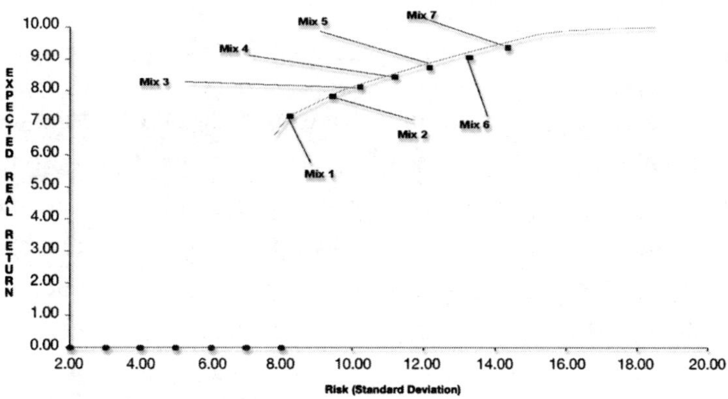

www.wmmercer.com

Most investors have difficulty understanding the concept of the efficient frontier because they generally believe that if they take on more risk, they will have the opportunity for more reward, or if they reduce their risk, they must settle for less reward. This is simply not the case in either scenario. Had you proved it, you quite likely would have won the Nobel Prize.

This principle can be illustrated with the inside/outside straight analogy. A straight is a run of five cards of any suit, such as 3, 4, 5, 6, 7. An outside straight would be, for example, having the 4, 5, 6 and 7 but missing either the 3 or the 8. In this instance, you need to draw either a 3 or 8. An inside straight would be, for example, having the 3, 4, 6 and 7 but missing the 5, so you need to draw a 5 to complete the straight. Your chances of completing the straight are twice as great in an outside straight, but the reward is the same; so risk and reward are not a 1:1 ratio.

This means that most investors expose themselves to too much risk and do not maximize their returns, usually by trading individual stocks or by trading mutual funds. This translates to subindex returns or, worse, loss of capital. Modern portfolio theory solves this problem by thinking in terms of diversified investment portfolios, control of volatility and maximizing returns, and focusing on the long term rather than the short term.

Canada and United States—the Differences

In terms of investing, Canada differs in two significant ways from the United States and both of these differences affect portfolio construction. First, Canada's RRSP program, with a maximum $13,500 annual contribution, is more significant than the U.S. IRA (Individual Retirement Account) program, which allows only a $2,000 annual contribution. This allows Canadians to build much larger tax-deferred savings than most Americans. In fact, for most Canadians, RRSP contribution levels will consume all the available investment resources that a Canadian investor has available, making it for many, if not most, investors, the single most important investment vehicle outside their home.

The second significant difference between Canada and the United States pertains to the different tax treatment of mortgage interest. In Canada, because mortgage interest is not a deduction, most Canadians spend much of their savings paying off their mortgages and amassing wealth in their homes. This makes real estate the largest single asset class held by most Canadians. This is not the case in the United States, where mortgage deductibility is a prime tax-planning tool. For Canadians, this appropriate preoccupation with paying off the mortgage consumes all their investment attention until much later in life. This means that outside of their RRSPs, most Canadians have little or no real investment experience just when they need it most—during their peak earning years (during Opus 2, the second work), when they can divert the greatest portion of their earnings to savings and investing.

Keep in mind that your biggest asset class as a Canadian is likely to be real estate—your house. As discussed earlier, in Canada slightly more than half of all homes have no mortgages, thus making the family home and real estate the largest single asset class for most Canadian investors.

This is the reason that I wrote *Allen Clarke's Adventures in Investing, How to Create Wealth and Keep It*—so I could provide the information for you when you needed this information most, during Opus 2, the second work. So let's begin to build that perfect portfolio—the one that will build the wealth you deserve and act as the foundation for all your other financial endeavors. Where should we begin?

<u>STEP ONE</u>: Asset-class selection; getting the main players in place.

Getting the asset classes correct is your first and most important priority. The main issue here is to get the main classes in place: U.S.

equities, Canadian equities, foreign equities and fixed income. Once the main ones are in place, you're 90% there. You can also consider additional asset classes such as small-cap Canadian, small-cap U.S., real estate, precious metals, commodities, foreign fixed income, emerging markets, cash or T-bills, country/continent funds such as Japan or Europe, or sector funds such as technology or e-commerce, to name a few. Regardless of which additional funds you add, once you have the main ones, the additions do not add appreciably to the efficiency of the portfolio. Of these, U.S. real estate is an important consideration but not in Canada for the reasons just outlined, and commodities, which are often countercyclical to the main markets, can often help. Of all the choices, I believe that U.S. small cap deserves consideration next.

All asset classes do not perform well at all times, nor do they all do poorly at the same time. If one asset class goes up while another goes down, this is known as a negative correlation and is the main reason for selecting more than one asset class. Since it is not possible to choose which asset class will do best in advance, diversification is necessary to ensure a return as well as reduce volatility. For this reason it is important to diversify: if one asset class does poorly, another asset class in your portfolio will do well and overall you will net a positive return and lower volatility. Just because the U.S. market is up doesn't mean the Canadian, Japanese or European markets are also up. Over the year ending December 31, 1999, Japanese equities have averaged an incredible 52.55%, the U.S. S&P 500 21.04%, Europe 9.60% and Canada 31.71%, yet over the last 10 years Japan has averaged only 1.52%, the U.S. 18.21%, Europe 17.04% and Canada 10.55%. Japan is a good example of a large asset class that has not behaved as anyone might have expected.

"The reverse side also has a reverse side."

Japanese proverb

Each asset class has its own fundamental characteristics. Historically, it will have produced a specific rate of return (percentage), had a certain level of volatility (highs and lows) and, most importantly, had a predictable relationship to other asset classes (correlation). Each additional asset class that you select for your portfolio should have good long-term returns, but a perfect additional asset class would have an exact negative correlation to other asset classes to have the maximum effect in reducing volatility and ensuring a return. Of course, the perfect asset class does not exist so we use several and aim for the best result.

The Influence of Cash

Several things are definitely not asset classes, the most important of which is cash. If you occasionally need funds, feel free to hold some cash, but trying to time the markets by going to cash is a futile endeavor. If you're in cash, you're out of the markets—and the markets are where wealth is created. In our lifetime, the markets have been and will continue to be in a long-term uptrend. Professional managers seldom, if ever, go to cash. They are paid to be in the market, not to sit on the sidelines. In fact, having even a little cash over a long period can reduce performance; this is commonly referred to as "the friction of cash." If the markets are going up by 15% and cash returns only 6%, the money manager is penalized 9% for any cash that he or she holds.

Many managers who feel the need for some cash for liquidity purposes may use futures contracts to replicate the markets for the cash portion that they hold just to reduce the friction of cash. As discussed earlier, going to cash is one thing, but getting back into the market at the bottom so you can benefit from your move to cash is another. I can tell you from experience that this is extremely difficult to do. After all, the negative sentiment that got you to go into cash lingers there and weighs heavily on your ability to switch to a positive view of the market and reinvest the cash. Market timing is a mug's game; only people at cocktail parties have ever been successful at it. For all practical purposes, cash is not a viable asset class.

Your House as an Asset Class

Keep in mind that, as a Canadian, your biggest asset class is likely to be real estate—your home. Your home is a special kind of asset class. At a recent seminar, a man asked whether it was wise to mortgage his house to invest. Someone had encouraged him to "use the equity he had accumulated to create more wealth" by using the cash he would receive from mortgaging his house to buy stocks. It wasn't really a question that I was prepared for, despite the fact that some people recommend this approach. Although I understand the tax implications, the write-offs and all the arguments in favor of doing so, in the split second I had to respond I answered, "No."

"Why not?" he asked.

"Because I sleep there." I explained. This is the response you get when your feelings override the numbers. Now that I have had more time to think about it, I would refine my answer. I think it's okay to borrow against your *house* to invest, but not against your *home*. If you view your house simply as real estate—that it's an investment and only an investment—then borrowing against it, levering up to buy stocks and receiving the tax deduction is probably a defendable concept. However, if you think of your house as the place where your children grow up, from where your daughter has her first date, where birthday parties are held, where you sat and shared dinner with your family and settled all the troubles of the world, where you seek refuge from the world at large, then using it as collateral to trade securities seems less than a good idea.

STEP TWO: Asset-class selection; don't let the bad guys in.

All the hard work of asset-class selection can be quickly undone or damaged by losing your focus and "letting the bad guys in." Although you might be pushed or motivated to go the extra bit, the best advice is: don't. Foreign fixed income, for example, historically has been unable to add much additional performance, but it does introduce new, undefined currency risks. This is an example where risk is introduced without the accompanying rewards. Similarly, emerging markets have done well in recent years, but it's a volatile asset class; last year, the asset class was up 9.6% and over two years it was up 19.1%, but on a three-year basis it is –2.7% ending June 30, 2000, so after three years an investor still does not have a positive return. Several years of double-digit losses can do a lot of damage, and the risk may not warrant it. Inclusion of such assets may be inappropriate, particularly if you are trying to time its inclusion.

Just as an aside, horses are not an asset class. I myself have dodged the bullet when it comes to horses. My broker friend calls, "Allen, we're buying a horse."

"We are?" I say.

"Absolutely. You, me, three other guys, up to $10,000 each. I have a friend, we're going to an auction, he's picking the horse, he will take care of us."

"Okay, I'm in."

Not that I had much choice. Losing money is one thing, but the thought of being left out when the nag wins the Triple Crown is too much to bear. The next day, I am thinking, "Great. Not only am I about to buy a horse, I am going to own it with four other guys, none of whom know anything about horses." A few weeks go by; I have completely forgotten about the horse—suppressed is probably a better term.

My friend calls: "Allen: good news, bad news." He sounds disappointed.

"Okay, give me the good news first."

"We picked the right horse."

"And the bad news?" I hesitate to ask. I'm thinking that it's going to cost me a fortune or, worse, maybe we bought two horses.

"He went for a lot more than we had expected and we couldn't buy him."

"No," I said, "that's the good news." And we never talked about horses again.

STEP THREE: Diversify by manager style; get good managers.

Your next step involves selecting the manager of the asset class itself. Here you must decide among value versus growth versus momentum or sector/industry weighting versus country weighting.

As I mentioned earlier, building a portfolio is analogous to the three stages involved in making a cake. First, you must choose ingredients, which equates to the asset-class selection. And then you must ensure that the best quality of the ingredients is selected, which equates to the selection of money managers for the asset classes. And finally you must combine these ingredients in just the right way, which equates to the asset allocation. Of all three activities, the choice of asset classes is the most important, the asset allocation is second, and selection of the money managers, while important, is the least important of the three.

> "The men who can manage men, manage the men who manage only things, and the men who can manage money manage all."
>
> *Will Durant*

Manager Style Slippage

The key point is to choose a manager who does exactly what he or she is hired to do. Unfortunately, managers are often tempted to do two things that damage performance. First, some managers will let cash build up in the account attempting to market-time, that is, waiting for a pullback to deploy the cash at what they hope will be lower stock prices. This increases the friction of cash and lowers performance. Beware of managers who practice closet market-timing.

Second, when their specific management style is out of favor for some time, as has been the case with value managers of late, these managers may make subtle changes to management styles. This is called "style slippage" and it clearly indicates that the manager has lost faith in the correctness of his or her methodology. Style slippage is a bad thing and can ruin all the hard work you applied to asset allocation and endeavoring to get on to the efficient frontier. Letting a manager use your money to redesign his or her methodologies is not conducive to your returns. Style slippage is clearly grounds to fire a money manager.

In the winter of 1999–2000 and the spring of 2000, it was not uncommon to see articles with titles such as "Is Warren Buffett Yesterday's Man?" or "The New Economy Is No Place for Value Managers." At the time, Opus 2 was using Beutel Goodman as our value manager—arguably one of a handful of true value managers in Canada. On March 15 Beutel was down more than 6% in the portfolio, and investors and board members were urging me to consider replacing Beutel. However, I have been through this before, as have the senior guys at Beutel, and in the last conversation I find out that they have just lost an account. Great, I thought, we have to be getting closer to their moment in the sun; the worse the news is, the more I am willing to hang in. Two months later, on May 15, the Beutel Canadian Value Fund was up more than 8%, a 15% positive swing in 60 days. That's an annualized two-month return of over 90%, and as the chart below illustrates, it skated every one of the Opus 2 portfolios on-side into positive territory, when most major indices were in negative territory.

This is a prime example of the importance of diversification by management style preserving capital during a very volatile period. April 14, 2000, saw a 700-point range of movement on the Dow, but the portfolios—thanks to style diversification and Beutel—stayed positive. So when the market resumed its appreciation in June, July and August, the Opus 2 portfolios were able to participate with full capital and went to new highs while others tried to regain the losses of April and May. This is so significant because it's all about preserving capital.

Opus 2 Portfolios for April & May 2000

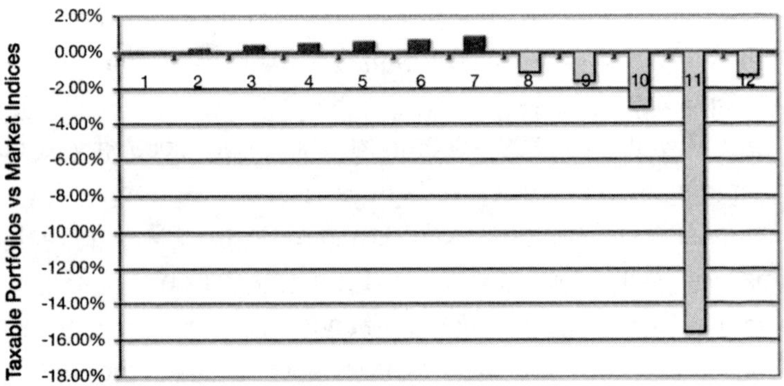

www.opus2direct.com/portperf_april.htm

So now, I am thinking about the poor pension advisor and the guys on the pension board who probably replaced that value manager with a growth manager just weeks before value gives them a 15% pop. Meanwhile, growth takes it in the ear, and these guys are supposed to know better.

Remember the problem that the brother who loses 8% had in catching up to the other brother who was up 8%? This is the same situation, just wrapped in a different set of circumstances. Diversification by management style is important because it reduces volatility and helps preserve capital, and thus enhances returns. This important step of manager diversification is often overlooked as simply involving too much work.

Today, far too much emphasis is placed on short-term performance—how a fund performed last month, last quarter or last year. Ignore this information because there is no predictability to short-term performance; in fact, it may be a better predictor of poor performance. Above-average performance is just that—above the average, an aberration. If you are attracted to this situation it is likely that you will buy just as the fund regresses to the mean—in other words, as it delivers lower performance, more normal performance, and perhaps even negative performance, in order to deliver normal returns over the long term.

Look for good managers with good long-term performance. If you are doing this by selecting a mutual fund, you should not care whether the fund is new as long as the manager of the fund has a good long-term (i.e., three- to five-year) track record. Many advisory services follow only funds with three- to five-year track records, which is fine, but many of these great managers start new funds that don't appear in these recommended categories for years, yet they still represent great opportunities.

Chasing Short-Term Performance

Chasing short-term performance is a clear recipe for disaster. Performance ebbs and wanes and flows in unpredictable patterns. Buying a fund just after it has posted exceptional results is like arriving at a party just at its peak—things quickly start to deteriorate, all the fun people have left, the food is gone and the ice is melting. The performance that initially attracted you to the fund is very likely to be over as the fund cycles into a period of normalized returns, which are obviously lower than its immediate past, because no one sector or investment style outperforms all others all the time and periods of unusually high performance are usually followed by periods of lower and often below-normal rates of return. You are most likely to be the investor who is down 8%. In fact, you will be lucky to be down only 8%.

> "Nobody goes there anymore; it's too busy."
> *Yogi Berra*

I raise this issue because near-past historic high rates of return are the principal subject of most mutual fund advertising. Accompanying each of these ads, however, is a disclaimer stating that "past performance does not guarantee future performance." These disclaimers typically go unheeded—much like the health warnings on cigarette packages. The reality is that if a fund has had a period of exceptional performance sufficient to warrant an advertisement, that fund is likely to be nearing a pullback. In fact, searching out the funds of good managers who have recently done poorly, while much more difficult, is a more sound strategy than buying funds that have recently had exceptional performance.

Each money management firm has many managers trained in, if not the architects of, the particular philosophy of the founding chief investment officer (CIO). It isn't necessary to have that person specifically manage your money as long as the philosophy is sound, and the acting CIO has some gray hair and has been through at least one bear market. The forces of evil are out there, in the form of advertisements tempting you with near-past abnormally high rates of return. You must be strong; do not slip over to the dark side. Remember that in order to protect capital you need good, experienced managers. The experience of the manager is critical—not just the age of the fund; there is nothing wrong with a new fund without a two-, three- or five-year track record if it is managed by an experienced manager with a good long-term track record. On the flip side, however, there may be something inherently wrong with a fund with a five- or 10-year track record, because it is not uncommon for a fund to change managers so the track record of the fund may not be the track record of the present manager. Since many fund evaluation services concentrate only on the fund and not on the management of the fund, such services will report on funds with long-term records regardless of management changes and will not report on funds with less than two- or three-year track records.

Value Managers and High Tech

Having said this, I do not have a problem with managers who evolve over time and adapt to fundamental changes in the market structure. Today, 30% of the broad-based markets are high tech. Many value managers have not done well lately as high tech represents such a significant portion of the market and these managers' traditional measures of value, basically P/E ratios, do not find value in this high-tech sector. Thus, these managers have not participated in the appreciation of this sector, which represents 30% of the market, and have consequently suffered considerably lower returns.

Meanwhile, other value managers, such as Opus 2's Global Alliance of San Francisco, rather than sit on the sidelines for 30% of the market, have adapted their methodology to root out value in such sectors where traditional value-evaluation methods will not work. These managers have adopted the use of the "relative price-to-sales ratio," a more cash-flow-based analysis with remarkable results.

The value managers who have not adopted this approach typically label it "style slippage" and frown upon the practice. And yet most value managers apply a different P/E measure to, say, pulp and paper stocks than they do to financial stocks. Thus, it seems reasonable that a different set of criteria would be applied to high tech than to other sectors. However, many value managers are reluctant to do this because the valuation difference between traditional sectors and the high-tech sector is so much greater than between pulp and paper and financials. Yet, if we were to look at a value manager's portfolio in the 1940s or 1950s, it would have contained a number of railway stocks, which represented a significant portion of that market. However, today, these managers are ignoring the high-tech sector of the market because it fails to meet traditional evaluations. So, the debate continues: is it style slippage or is it adaptation? I believe that it is clearly an adaptation to the evolution of the capital markets.

> "If you want things to remain the same around here, things are going to have to change."
>
> *Anonymous*

<u>STEP FOUR</u>: Set the asset allocation; don't get fancy, close counts.

Now that we have chosen our asset classes and the right manager, we must put it all together with asset allocation. If performance comes from asset-class selection, then consistency of returns, capital protection and control of volatility or risk come from asset allocation. Together we get the best of both worlds—high consistent returns and capital protection with low volatility.

The NorthWest Quadrant

What professionals call dwelling in the NorthWest Quadrant is what it is all about. If you look at a chart of risk, with the horizontal axis increasing to the right and returns on the vertical axis increasing as you move up, and you divide the chart into quadrants, the upper-left or NorthWest Quadrant represents high returns and low risk. To a professional money manager, having a portfolio that's in the NorthWest Quadrant is analogous to finding the Holy Grail.

Now that you have chosen the asset classes, to create a portfolio you must decide on the percentages of each. Typically a firm such as William M. Mercer or Towers Perrin or Frank Russell or Garmaise, using algorithms based on defining the efficient frontier, uses historic

Relative Risk and Returns of Different Investment Styles

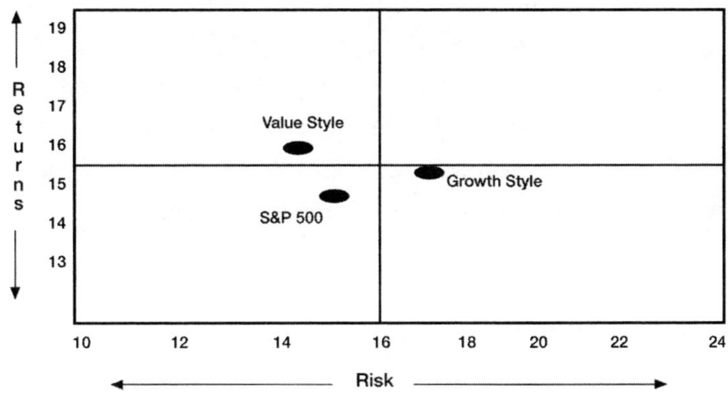

volatility measures and rates of returns to make intellectually driven assumptions about what these future returns and volatilities might be. Then they feed these assumptions into the mathematical models and select a number, usually 9-3 portfolios that lie on the efficient frontier, and offer a range of choice.

Asset Allocation

This is not an exact science, as many would lead you to believe. The efficient frontier is constantly shifting, as are the historic measurements of volatility and rates of return. If an investor were to take four major asset classes, such as U.S. equities, Canadian equities, Canadian fixed income and overseas equities, and put 25% of his or her assets in each, the investor would have a fairly efficient portfolio that would likely do very well. This is not to say that further refinement in the asset selection and asset allocation does not move the portfolio further into the NorthWest Quadrant, and add to the level of efficiency. It does. However, once the major asset classes are represented, improvements in efficiency are marginal.

The following is the Opus 2 Direct level 6 portfolio, which epitomizes this approach. Representing four asset classes including a number of various management styles designed by William M. Mercer to lie on the efficient frontier, it dwells in the NorthWest Quadrant. There must be a balance between the complexities and added costs of additional asset classes and the marginal improvements in efficiency of the portfolios. I believe that this trade-off exists somewhere in the four to six asset classes, two to three management style areas, of which the portfolio below is right in the middle.

Opus 2 Portfolio Allocation

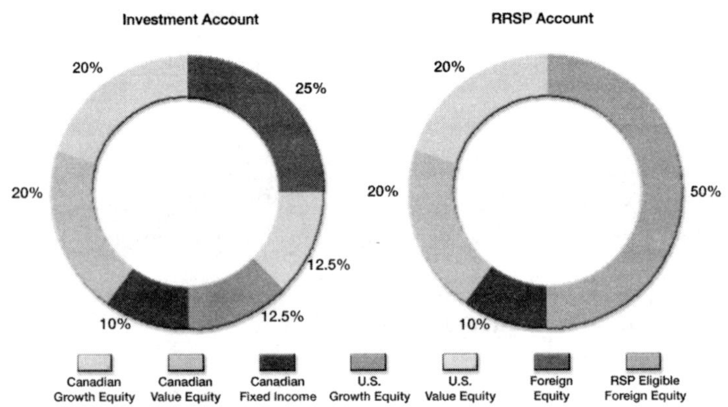

www.opus2direct.com/models.html

One note of interest is that Canada, which represents less than 2% of the capitalization of the industrialized world, is always overrepresented in Canadian asset-allocation models, because this is the country where we live. After all, it is prudent to have the largest representation reflect the currency and the economy in which the investor dwells. Expanding on this logic, I would argue that most U.S. portfolio asset allocations would be better off with a somewhat disproportionate exposure to Canada as an asset class simply because we are their largest trading partner and have the largest economic external effect on their economy; 5% to 10% would be appropriate. Over the last year, ending June 30, 2000, the Dow is down by 4.51 while the TSE is up 47.4. The addition of Canada as an asset class would have offered most U.S. portfolios a nice diversification and enhanced returns over the last year.

And don't overlook the importance of currency risk. Underlying any foreign asset class is that country's currency risk, which can easily erase any capital stock appreciation you may gain.

STEP FIVE: Maintain your portfolio with strategic asset allocation.

Strategic asset allocation involves setting the asset mix and leaving it alone, but investors, being human, often can't leave well enough alone. So once the portfolio is in place, they start to think about predicting which asset class might do better than the others in the near future and over-weighting in that asset class to boost performance. This is known as tactical asset allocation.

The principle behind strategic allocation is there is no doubt that one asset class will outperform another in the near future, but it is impossible to predict which asset class that will be. The activity of shifting weightings in asset classes underweights you in overperforming asset classes as often as it overweights you in the overperforming classes. There is no advantage in trying to predict short-term market fluctuations.

Tactical Asset Allocation

Research has also been done in tactical style allocation, trying to predict whether value management or growth management will do better in the near term. Such research has yielded mixed results. In the United States, a number of tactical-asset products profess to add performance by shifting asset classes. But even for specialized institutional investors the long-term advantage is small—1/4 to 1/2 percent—and certainly not a recommended goal for retail investors.

In 1998–99, many Canadians looked south to what they believed were greener pastures; the Dow and the S&P 500 had been outperforming the TSE by a good amount for several years and in 1999 there occurred very high redemptions in Canadian equities in favor of U.S. equity purchases. In the year ending June 30, 2000, as we have just mentioned, the Dow was down 4.8 while the TSE was up 47.4. So this attempt to predict which asset class will next outperform the other resulted in a considerable loss of performance for the tactical asset allocators.

In the world of professional managers, those who attempt tactical asset allocation do so in moderation with the goal of adding just a few basis points of performance. Usually it is a committee decision and, after reviewing the various asset classes, they may decide to underweight bonds by 5%, bringing the bond holdings to 35%, and increase the equity holdings by 5%, bringing them to 65%. There is never any talk of going 100% cash or exiting the United States in favor of Canada; there is only talk of moderate shifts.

Companies such as William M. Mercer are often hired to test the activities of money managers' "attribution analysis" to see which activities, such as country weighting, stock selection, asset allocation and style allocation, add value. As often as not, even professional money managers cannot add value by tactical asset allocation.

Violent tactical asset allocation—going to a high percentage of cash and waiting for a market correct—is a common practice among retail investors who manage their own accounts. Yet, managers such as Sir John Templeton, Peter Lynch and Warren Buffett, the very best in the business, are never heard to say, "I am going to cash." Again, this reiterates my point that if you want to have wealth, you must behave like those people who have wealth, and they don't try to market-time by going to cash.

Many brokers and planners do not favor strategic asset allocation because it diminishes their role and the opportunity to add perceived value by recommending changes and triggering new commissions. So, many of them look for an opportunity to switch funds, as was the case in 1998–99 from Canadian to U.S. equities to add perceived value and trigger new commissions. It is difficult to understand how not doing anything adds value, but clearly in the case of asset allocation, less is better.

Thus tactical asset allocation is inappropriate for most retail clients who lack the skills or discipline to apply a tactical methodology with any reasonable chance of success. In fact, understanding the retail client's inclination for excess in tactical asset allocation (such as going 100% to cash or all into the United States out of Canada) is almost certain to lead to diminished capital and lower returns. Set an appropriate mix and leave it alone; rebalance to the prescribed asset allocation once every nine to twelve months. You have better things to do than try to predict future asset-class performance.

STEP SIX: Maintain focus and stay the course.

Today, everything is instant. From microwave popcorn to face-lifts, everyone is looking for immediate results. CNBC broadcasts news 24 hours a day; if it's happening, it's reported within minutes, perhaps seconds, but wealth isn't created within such a short period. Minutes, days and months are inappropriate time frames for wealth creation.

> "Waiting gives a man a chance to practice patience."
>
> *Benjamin Franklin*

When I was a child my family regularly traveled to Florida in our car. Our car was a Hudson and the trip took three days from start to finish. We discussed the trip for weeks and both my brother and I knew all the details—including the fact that the trip would take three days. Yet we weren't on the road for more than an hour when we asked if we were there yet, and I'm sure that another hour didn't pass before we asked again. Today's investor is like that child in the backseat of a car on a long trip.

The Hudson Motor Car Company was started on February 24, 1909. In 1951 Tim Flock won the NASCAR championship in a Hudson Hornet. The company reached peak production of 43,000 units in 1951 and thereafter declined until the nameplate died in 1957.

I recently attended a meeting with some technical people during which we discussed linking the daily closing prices of Opus 2 Direct pools to a wireless technology so that our clients could receive daily updates to their portfolios valued daily by 4:30 p.m. on their pagers and Palm Pilots. Yet, do investors who own and believe in investment portfolios really need daily updates? Arguably they need ongoing access on a 24-7 basis to current updated data, but they only need to access such information on a needs basis—such as weekly or monthly. Having access to correct and current information is completely different from being fed data daily about a long-term process. Wealth creation takes time; checking stock prices over the Internet three times a day is like asking if you're there yet.

A well-designed investment portfolio is more than an investment philosophy—it is a quality-of-life issue; it provides peace of mind. An investment portfolio removes the daily requirements of trading stocks and managing a trading account. It lets you focus on your real work or play effort, and not be distracted by an activity where you are less or even ill prepared for success. It reduces the stress associated with risk to capital, and the stress of the responsibilities of direct investments. An investment portfolio is simply a better way for an investor to move from point A to point B, and point B is wealth creation.

This whole process takes time, but along the way there are temptations. Don't be misled into shifting asset classes, chasing performance or adding new exotic asset classes. Stay the course. In an era of instant everything, give your investment portfolio the time it needs to do the job it was designed to do: create wealth.

Now that you are convinced that you should manage your money like the wealthy folk because that's how they got to be wealthy folk, where do you go to get that perfect portfolio?

Find an Investment Portfolio Provider

Although many planning firms and brokerage houses now offer fee-based portfolio products, which deal with the investment process, many of the brokers and planners within those companies do not offer these products. Rather, many brokers and planners remain transaction-based so they are still primarily interested in trading individual stocks or mutual funds. So, remember, it's caveat emptor.

> "Firms should move from product management to process management if they are to remain competitive."
>
> *Jack Welch*

In the United States and, to a lesser degree, in Canada, some firms now deliver these investment processes directly to clients. They bypass brokers and planners completely in order to lower fees considerably. Since investment portfolios are designed and managed at the fund-company level, there is less need for the value-added component of a broker or planner. This process, whereby the broker and planner are bypassed and the client goes directly to the manufacturer, is called "disintermediation" and is a hotly contested area within the investment community. But, in the United States, more than 40% of mutual funds are successfully delivered by this direct method as opposed to only 5% in Canada. Direct purchase is now a viable alternative for fee-based investment portfolios. Remember: lower fees mean better performance, shorter doubling times and greater wealth creation.

If you are hungry for seafood, you go to a restaurant that specializes in seafood; but if you are interested in steak, you don't go to a seafood restaurant. Seems simple. But if you're interested in a fee-based portfolio, you must not only be careful to go to a financial firm that offers fee-based products, but also to find a broker or planner within that firm who deals in and believes in portfolio management. Whether you go direct or via a planner or broker, firms have different cultures, such as a transaction culture or a money management culture. You want a firm steeped in a money management culture and an individual within that firm who believes passionately in modern portfolio theory. Getting this fit right from the start will manifest itself in a productive relationship; getting this wrong will waste time and delay capital appreciation. This decision is extremely critical to your financial success. Several interviews and sound research up front will more than pay off.

Doing It Yourself

If you decide to do it yourself, then your basic portfolio building block will be existing mutual funds, and a number of services will allow you to get information directly to make a more informed choice.

www.globefund.com
www.excite.ca/money
www.morningstar.ca
www.fundlibrary.com
www.investment.com
www.opus2direct.com
www.imoney.com
www.quicken.ca
www.stockhouse.ca

First, since you will be rebalancing and adjusting the asset mix over time you must purchase these mutual funds in the correct manner in order to maintain liquidity and avoid high MERs and unnecessary fees and commissions. Remember: fees reduce your performance. According to *Investor Economics,* in the first quarter of 2000 76% of funds were still being purchased with back-end loads, funds that must be held for periods of up to seven years to avoid additional commissions. Since the average holding period of funds is decreasing and some data suggest the period to be shorter than three years, these early sales trigger an additional 5% to 6% deferred sales charge. Such early sales result in total average annual fees of a Canadian equity fund of not the advertised 2.4% average MER, but an all-in cost of 3.5% to 4.5%. Such fee levels will negatively affect the performance of the component funds and thus the performance of the overall portfolios.

Historically, broker-planners have sold deferred sales charge funds (for which they receive an immediate commission payment of 5%), but if the investor holds the funds for typically six or seven years, he or she would pay no other commissions but would be subject to declining commission penalties for early sale of the fund. Regardless, however, the investor still pays the annual MER. With shorter holding periods this back-end fee structure is coming increasingly under attack.

To keep your costs of these mutual fund building blocks as low as possible and also maintain liquidity, you must purchase front-end load mutual funds and insist on a zero front-end load. To further reduce the cost, if you are doing the portfolio construction, you may wish to go direct without the aid of a broker or planner, to access funds without loads and with lower MERs.

> "Apply yourself. Get all the education you can, but then, by God do something. Don't just stand there, make it happen."
>
> *Lee Iacocca*

Regardless of which funds you buy and which way you purchase them, simply follow the procedures outlined in this chapter. Select your asset classes, choose your managers by asset class and style, and choose a mutual fund representing each category. Do not be influenced by short-term performance and avoid funds with very high recent returns. Remember: way up, way down. In the end you will have approximately four to nine mutual funds representing domestic, U.S. and foreign asset classes as well as both value and growth managers in the major asset classes, and perhaps a fixed-income manager or one or two specialty managers such as small cap, high tech or resource sector. Remember that the choice of a bad specialty fund because of the high risk usually associated with them can negate all your hard work of designing the core asset allocation. Most investors do not understand the importance of style diversification and don't bother with it, so be certain that with at least two of the major asset classes you have chosen both a value and a growth manager, perhaps even a momentum player. Remember to purchase the funds as front load with zero front load, to avoid penalties if you later adjust the portfolio.

Recently I encountered a number of investors who have 15 or more mutual funds in their accounts. This is gross overdiversification and leads to less than index performance. Four to nine well-chosen funds are sufficient to diversify a portfolio and yet also allow it to fully participate in the major markets.

It doesn't end here for those who have chosen to do it themselves. They must continually monitor the individual fund managers and their performance; evaluate the role of special sector funds; be willing to change managers or funds if the performance is bad or if there is style slippage or if the sector becomes inappropriate; and rebalance when appropriate. All these functions require a different skill set and are performed by professionals within the firms that offer portfolio solutions.

Summary

STEP ONE: Asset-class selection; getting the main players in place.

STEP TWO: Asset-class selection; don't let the bad guys in.

STEP THREE: Diversify by manager style; get good managers.

STEP FOUR: Set the asset allocation; don't get fancy, close counts.

STEP FIVE: Maintain your portfolio with strategic asset allocation.

STEP SIX: Maintain focus and stay the course.

In most cases, investors do not do this alone. They will likely choose a portfolio offering such as Opus 2 Direct or seek advice from a financial planner or broker where the chores of asset-class selection and manager selection and monitoring are done by professionals. In this case you want to look for a portfolio service or product that incorporates these features. Be focused in your search for the right investment portfolio provider. Don't be lured over to transaction-based accounts, and ask about the total fees involved. In particular, don't tolerate back-end loads or penalties of any kind so ask for full disclosure on the fees. It's your money and your wealth we are creating.

The problem with portfolio investing is that it doesn't generate any great cocktail-party stories. There is nothing sexy about portfolio design:

"Ernie, last week I rebalanced my portfolio."

"Really, Bert?"

"Oh yes, I added 2.5% international and lowered my fixed-income exposure by an equal amount."

"Great, Bert, that must move you up on the efficient frontier."

"Absolutely Ernie, I am perfectly positioned now." Assuming that you're not asleep by now, you can see how a discussion about portfolio construction can't compare to a good trading story.

Regardless, this is how wealthy people manage their money and portfolios create wealth—and that makes for a great story. So before we move on to the chapter you have all been waiting for, the chapter on trading, don't forget that the investment portfolio must be the foundation of your wealth creation.

4 "Before You Enter the Pool, a Few Safety Rules"

Now that we've discussed investing, let's turn our attention to trading. One trait that all traders need is optimism—good traders are never short on optimism. Over the past 20 years, I feel certain that I have, in my own account, made most of the cardinal sins of trading.

> "It's the lure of easy money, it has very strong appeal."
>
> *Smugglers Blues*

There is no other way to describe it: "It's the lure of easy money." Trading is all of that and more. For our purposes, we must view it as a means of wealth creation and, as such, there are proven ways to improve your chances of a profitable result. First, trading must be done in association with a properly constructed portfolio as described in the previous chapter. For this reason, the chapter on portfolio design preceded this one on trading. Let's also not forget protection of capital, and the long-term nonreversible negative effect of diminished capital. The risk embodied in trading should be restricted to a maximum of 25% of total investment capital.

Strangely enough, when it comes to trading, it's been my experience that brokers often do a better job for their clients than for themselves. That's because, in most cases, they're willing to ignore normal due diligence when it applies to themselves.

In 1981, when I returned to Ottawa after the McLeod training program in Toronto, one of the senior brokers took me aside.

"Clarkeee," he says (nicknames are common in the brokerage business and unfortunately the recipient seldom has any input as to the selection), "don't bother me with phone calls unless there is something in it for me, like a stock idea that can make me money, and, oh, by the way, good luck." This gives an outsider an idea of how friends are made in the business. It's not that he was being impolite or insensitive. It's just the high value of time and the pervasive culture of money.

Successful brokers, by definition, place an enormous value on time because their time equates directly to money. A broker lives for the phone to ring. It's a fundamental Pavlovian response: bell rings, dog gets fed; phone rings, broker gets money. I can't honestly say that I have ever seen a broker salivate when the phone rings, but, to this day, when the phone rings in my office, the old response kicks in.

Over the years, I've swapped ideas with colleagues many times, some successful, some not, but always with the best intentions of making clients money. But of all these ideas, three stand out above the others.

The day before I was leaving for Ottawa, one of the senior brokers took me aside. It's like the classic "Plastics" moment in *The Graduate*. I think if there was a remake of *The Graduate* today they would get Paul Allen to stand in and the word of advice would be "Bandwidth," but that is a topic for another book.

"I've got one word for you," he said. "Are you paying attention?" At this point, I was all ears. I feel he's about to reveal the location of the Holy Grail and I don't want to miss a word.

"Turbo Resources," he said in a hushed voice. I thought, that's two words. And then he repeated it: "Turbo Resources."

He continued. As you know, execution is everything. "Go to Ottawa, call every wealthy person you can find and get them into Turbo Resources. This and this alone will make your career." Armed with this proprietary knowledge and the confidence of the source, I was off. Not since I bundled up all my possessions and went off to college had I felt so certain that my course was right.

This is 1981–82. The price of oil is over $50 a barrel in 1982. Oil is on everyone's mind and in everyone's account. (I was going to say portfolio rather than account, but in those days, a portfolio was an esoteric concept at the retail level and that was the last chapter.) Unfortunately, everything that made oil a great investment changed in the next six months and the only thing that saved me and my clients from disaster was that the oil market collapsed, taking Turbo with it before I could actually convince enough clients to buy the stock. This was not the case for many of the established brokers. Nothing can be potentially more dangerous to their net worth than a stock story they really believe in, and, as I mentioned earlier, they often do worse for themselves than their clients. Turbo was no exception, as the brokers' losses far exceeded those of their clients. It wasn't a bad idea; it was bad timing. Herein lies the all-important element of trading: timing.

> "If everyone is talking about something, that's the time to sell."
>
> *George Lindemann*

Brokers were synonymous with traders because, in the early 1980s, brokers were traders—not portfolio managers. Today, many brokers are portfolio managers and operate much like small asset management companies within the firms for which they work. But again, we explored that fully in the last chapter. Good brokers are like those weighted plastic inflatable dolls. You keep knocking them down and they keep bouncing back. The guys at Turbo, however, are down and they aren't coming back up. But even with this setback, I'm back at it, as is my friend, and just as enthusiastic as ever.

Which brings me to my second story. I'm more experienced and now we talk again. "Uranium," he whispered. The worse the stock idea, the more likely the source is to whisper. He continues: "There's a mine in Northern Ontario, so rich that the digging equipment is radioactive."

In disbelief, I asked, "Radioactive?"

"Absolutely," he insisted. "They're worried about disposing of the digging equipment. It glows in the dark."

Should make it easy to find at night, I think. Then the clincher: "The workers have to wear lead suits."

Well, as soon as I hear this, I put some in my account. The next time I talk to him, there is only one item of conversation: do I have enough? Sure enough I do own more than enough, because the bloom came off uranium, like three-day-old potato salad, and the stock, as they say, went south. Enthusiasm overcame reason and due diligence. Herein lies another all-important element of trading: greed.

> "Controlled greed can give you an edge. It's a good thing for you and your money. Uncontrolled greed will ruin most investors."
>
> *Jesse Livermore*

Time passes. The phone rings. This time, no whisper, just, "I think Polysar is undervalued. I think their earnings are going to be better than anyone expects." So I made some inquiries and crunched some numbers. Then I called back.

"I think you're low; the numbers could be even better." In fact, "The earnings might not be far off what the stock price is." One times earnings is good, very good. This time, I bought for clients and myself, as does he. We couldn't believe that we'd figured this out and that no one else had. I'm nervous. Next time we talk, the stock is moving up but still within a good buying range.

"Are you sure about the earnings?" I asked. Later he called again, more excited this time.

"I think we're still low."

We continue to accumulate. The stock triples in price, pays a huge deemed dividend and sheds off a holding as additional shares. All was right with the universe. Reason and hard work prevailed and herein lies yet another all-important element in trading: information.

> "Investors operate with limited funds, and limited intelligence. They don't need to know everything. As long as they understand something better than others, they have an edge."
>
> *George Soros*

October 1987

October 1987. I am at my desk. I've got a horrible cold, but the Dow is down 500 points and I can't go home. The tape is running four hours late so all stock pricing is a guess at best. Trying to trade stocks when you don't know the prices is like hunting with Ray Charles.

A major client calls. "Sell everything," he says.

I advise against this. "What if this continues?" he asks.

Then I interrupt. "Well, the Dow's already at 1,500. Three more days of this and you can buy all of America for a dollar."

My advice seemed to work; he was content. Well, content wasn't the right word, but he stuck nonetheless. In fact, for the next three days I didn't trade. How can you trade if you don't know what the stock prices are? Because I didn't, and didn't use margin, I had no margin calls on any client accounts. Of course, I receive a margin call on my own account because, as I mentioned, like most brokers, I've tried stuff on myself that I'd never try on a client.

Eventually, the market settles and by year-end, it's back up a bit, but year to date, from January 1, 1987, to December 31, 1987, the Dow was up only about 8%. The only people who lost money were those who thought on a short-term basis and who reacted to the moment. This left me with one of the great revelations of my investment career: everyone has a plan for spending the money they're going to make and almost no one has a plan to write another check for the money they can lose. Unbridled optimism engenders a failure to plan. This leads me to another all-important element in trading: a two-way plan.

"They all have a plan till they get hit."
Mike Tyson

Before we begin to discuss *how* and *what* to trade, we need to first agree on *when* and in what *context* to trade. The retail trader almost always overlooks these important considerations. By context, I mean in relationship to your overall investment plan and within the parameters that you'll be setting.

Let's get one thing straight: trading is not a game. It is a means to an end. It is work designed to create wealth—nothing more, nothing less. You can't apply game philosophies to it, such as "it doesn't matter who wins or loses" or "honor in defeat." With trading, there is only one objective: success. When a game becomes an industry, such as pro football, new philosophies arise such as "winning is everything" and "no one remembers who came in second." This is as it should be when the main objective is to increase one's personal net worth.

Timing

When you should trade is the most misunderstood and ignored consideration, yet arguably it is the most important. In a nutshell, you should only trade if you believe you can win. It's not like hockey with the guys on Thursday night, where you're playing for the fun of it. If you applied a true trader philosophy to it, you would check out the other team and if they looked bigger and faster, you would put your gear back in your bag and slip out the back door.

In the retail world, you seldom see behavior befitting a professional trader. During the late 1980s, a broker friend of mine, who specialized in commodities, received a call from an inactive client who wanted to trade copper futures. He put the position with proper stops (meaning he put an order in when he buys to sell later should the price drop to a certain level in order to limit his loss), averaged up into the position (which means that as the position increases in price, he continues to buy more) and, a few weeks later, closed out the position with a $250,000 profit.

My broker friend presented him with numerous ideas and he's now "in the game," and begins to trade all sorts of commodities on an almost-daily basis and loses half the capital. Then he went back to what he knew, waiting for the right opportunity, that moment where everything is to his advantage, being professional.

Then he says, "I'm not interested. Don't call me. I'll let you know when I'm interested." Seven long months pass before the phone rings again. "Let's short orange juice," he suggested. Same thing, put the position on, put the stops in place, average up, sell out, take the profit, increase your net worth. He's up over $1 million. He has learned to choose his spots, wait for the right conditions that favor his success. He's becoming a professional.

This trader made all his money on only two profitable positions over an 18-month time frame, and, in the end, only two opportunities arose where the conditions so favored success that it warranted risk of capital. This will also be true for you. Probably no more than one or two great opportunities a year will present themselves. Most retail traders still talk about wanting to be in the game. This mind-set predisposes them to failure.

RULE #1. Trading is not a game. It's a business and, as such, you should only be actively in business when the conditions greatly favor your success.

"In this game, the market has to keep pitching but you don't have to swing. You can stand there with the bat on your shoulder for six months until you get a fat pitch."
Warren Buffett

Context

This answers the question of when and leads to the equally important issue of *context*. I have become more concerned about context since reading recent research that revealed that most day traders are using margin and that they expose their entire account to loss on each trade. A more prudent strategy, and the one I recommend, was recently outlined by Jonathan Clements in his December 14, 1999, *Wall Street Journal* article, "Building a Portfolio? Exploit your Weakness." He describes the importance of segmenting your account into a portfolio, in which you'd invest 60% to 80% of your money and 20% to 40% in trading, and then conducting your trading activities within the considerations of the whole investment portfolio.

Trading should not be done in isolation as the primary and sole activity within your investment strategy. A more professional and prudent strategy is to make trading an integral, but limited, part of your total investment strategy (such as 25%). This would be in association with and complementary to a diversified investment portfolio that comprises the principal portion of your investment account (such as 75%). Making trading the sole element of your investment strategy is not only unprofessional, but also foolhardy.

The next chapter discusses portfolio design in detail, but suffice it to say that a well-constructed portfolio is the key structure from which a professional trader launches his or her prudent trading strategy. And by prudent, we mean discreet use of margin and limitations on risk to principal.

RULE #2. Trading is an activity done in concert with your whole portfolio and should be restricted to a portion no greater than 25% of the whole.

Our orange-juice trader certainly did his homework and was ready to act with the proper execution techniques when opportunities presented themselves. This, of course, leads us to the next question—how do you recognize the opportunity and *how* do you trade when the opportunity occurs? Assuming that you have a proper portfolio as a base within your investment account, we're almost ready for our first trade.

Trading Opportunities

Ask yourself why would we go to all this trouble to trade an individual stock. If you're thinking of 10% returns, the risk that you incur trading individual stocks yourself is unwarranted and the probability of success is low. If that is your goal, then stock trading is not for you and your entire portfolio should be in a William M. Mercer–designed Opus 2 portfolio. Make no mistake, your goal here is to look for exceptional opportunities that come along rarely—positions that are likely to double, triple or quadruple in value. That's why we're doing such exhaustive and regimented research. This is clearly a high-risk, high-reward venture, which is why we have restricted it to 25% of the portfolio. As they say in the business, we're going elephant hunting.

Let's assume that you have an investment account worth $100,000, and $75,000 is sitting in a properly constructed portfolio, made up of Opus 2 Pools, and $25,000 is available to trade individual stock positions. So the first problem is choosing which stock(s). Most professional money managers have a very regimented process for selecting the stock they wish to purchase. In fact, most use a checklist. And so should you. On the following page are some of the common questions I've seen over the years on these screening sheets.

THE ELEPHANT'S NAME: SYMBOL: PRICE:

Company Profile: What does the company actually do, and what about it interests you?

First step:

- Find out whether any investment houses follow the stock and obtain and read their reports.
- Get a price volume chart history, which is available online from most investment houses.
- Find and read the latest six months of news releases or articles written about the company.

Then answer these key questions about the stock:

- Is it liquid enough to trade? (If no, stop now.)
- Is it a cyclical industry? Is it capital intense? Is it regulated?
- Are there institutional buyers or ownership?
- What is the ownership structure?
- Who are the principal shareholders?
- Are there any outstanding legal issues?
- What are the price-earnings and price-to-sales ratios?
- Growth rate and industry growth rate?
- What is the book value?
- What is the company's cash position and capital structure?
- What does the senior management team look like and how are they remunerated?
- Has there been any insider buying or selling?
- What's the competition like? What are the barriers to entry?
- What is its market share?
- What is the cash-flow history?

List the five most positive things about the company.

List the five most negative things about the company.

Define the key reason why the stock should increase in price.

Set Buying Range $_____ to $ ______ Set Selling Target Price $______

(Note: The selling price must be at least three times the average purchase price.)

"Spend at least as much time researching a stock as you would choosing a refrigerator."

Peter Lynch

Now you'll have a methodology and a plan. Customize this list to reflect your ideas and values, and to help you carry out your personal investment strategy. Be prepared to modify it as you find what works for you and what doesn't. Be creative and flexible in the application of this process.

At the end of the day, a stock never increases because there are more buyers than sellers—because there can *never* be more buyers than sellers. The number of buyers is always equal to the number of sellers and the movement of the price ensures that. What can and does happen is that either the buyers or sellers may show more enthusiasm and thus influence the price movement. When buyers are more willing to accept and hit the asking price than sellers are willing to accept and hit the bid price, also called the bid, then the price goes up and vice versa. But when the bell sounds, the number of buyers exactly equals the number of sellers.

When you finish your stock selection and subsequent research sheet, you must be convinced that at some time in the near future the buyers will demonstrate a sustainable enthusiasm for buying the stock, greater than the present owners will have for keeping the stock, for by definition they will become the sellers. If and when you feel this way, you can proceed with tempered enthusiasm.

"Buy when others are despondently selling and sell when others are greedily buying."

Mark Mobius

Negative Indicators

When I think of enthusiastic buyers, I can't help but remember the spring of 1980. My mother calls. "I am buying silver," she says. "I pick it up next week from the Bank of Nova Scotia."

"Pick it up?" I ask.

"Yes, I'm buying the real stuff, bullion."

"Who carries it for you?" I ask.

"Dad carries it to the car for me."

Well, this is what I call an enthusiastic buyer and I guess somewhere there was an equally enthusiastic seller. If there was ever a leading indicator of a short sale opportunity, this was it. But not even a broker can take the short side of a trade against his own mother—well, at least not this one.

Within a month, silver was at U.S.$50 an ounce and Bunker Hunt was facing the world's largest margin call, thanks to the Feds changing the margin rules midstream, and silver headed back down to $5 an ounce. Mom passed away a few years ago. Silver was still about $4.50 an ounce and she was still waiting for the price rebound. No sense in selling it now. The memories are worth more than the silver and who would carry it to the car?

My mother was one of the great negative leading indicators of the twentieth century. The time is the mid-1950s, my parents were running a corner-store garage in Kingston, Ontario, Clarke's Drive-In, and they are offered the Volkswagen dealership. "Who in Canada is going to buy a German car after the war?" she offered. I could have been running a VW car dealership driving a Porsche in Kingston today, if it hadn't been for World War II.

It doesn't stop there. A few years later, Tim Horton, then playing for the Toronto Maple Leafs, visits Mom and Dad. This is when people actually believed the Leafs had a shot at the Stanley Cup. He and my father sat at our kitchen table and they had coffee. Mom made it, and they all talked about Dad selling doughnuts—not just any kind of doughnuts but Tim Horton Donuts. Dad was big on doughnuts and had this great recipe for the old-fashioned style. They swapped stories and recipes and Tim tried to convince Mom and Dad to get into the Tim Horton Donuts business. "Who's going to sit around all day and drink coffee and eat doughnuts?" Mom asks. I could have been running a chain of Tim Horton doughnut shops in Eastern Ontario, driving a Porsche.

Investments Too Good to Be True

Research does not guarantee success. It is not always what it seems to be. It's just one of a number of trading tools that must be combined with proper trading techniques—techniques designed to cut losses and protect capital and let profits run and build capital. That's why, even after you have the right portfolio and you've decided on how much capital you want to expose to the risk of trading and you've selected a stock to trade, you must have actual trading skills to be successful, which leads me to an example of research gone awry.

At the height of the oil market in the 1980s, along came a 150-page report on Ocelot Energy entitled "A Stock in Transition." The stock was at $60+, and late one afternoon, every McLeod broker was tied into a direct call to the Australian outback via radiophone for a live report from the analysts right from the actual well site. It was 4 a.m. there, and we were all glued to the phones. Over the wire came the garbled report somewhat of the quality reminiscent of my first home-built crystal radio set, which, if you can remember, is just slightly better than two tin cans and a string. Thankfully, I never believed the Ocelot story, and shortly thereafter the stock began its agonizing decline (probably because of the weight of the research paper itself) and eventually traded at 50 cents.

"The price of a stock varies inversely with
the thickness of its research file."

Martin Sosnoff

However, when it came to the lure of the Arctic, particularly the Beaufort Sea oil exploration, I bought in. It was a time when oil was king, a time when everyone knew the Inuit names of the drill sites and the flow rates through a modified chock. The research and information were prodigious, but few of us knew what a modified chock was, nor spoke Inuit, and even fewer of us made money and kept it on these adventures. The oil boom of the early 1980s was a high drama in the Canadian resource sector. It's what being an entrepreneur is all about. It goes to the very roots of being Canadian. It was an important and wonderful adventure that I am happy to have been part of despite the fact that it did not add to my own or my clients' net worth.

This is clearly the kind of epic Canadian adventure that could have been put to rhyme by Robert Service or to song by Gordon Lightfoot and prevented the whole fascinating tale from bleeding into obscurity.

Special Trading Opportunities

Every day when a broker comes to work, especially those who do traditional trading, he or she needs an idea. Without an idea, brokers are dead in the water; there's no reason to call, no story to tell, no positions to trade, no revenue, no BMW.

It's the 1980s and I am looking for a good idea every waking minute of every day. One of my most profitable ones was my "junk-food strategy." I am drinking four Cokes a day, not counting the one for breakfast. A friend of mine owns six McDonald's restaurants and is doing okay, even better than okay, and a week doesn't go by that I don't get a craving for KFC. The world as I see it is being powered by junk food, although my friend with the McDonald's restaurants hates the term "junk food." He prefers "family dining," but as far as I'm concerned, if it's wrapped in paper, it's served to you in less than three minutes and you eat it with your hands, it's not fine dining.

So I put together a three-stock junk-food portfolio—Coke, PepsiCo and McDonald's. PepsiCo owns Frito Lay, KFC, Pizza Hut and Pepsi. If junk food hangs in there, we have all the bases covered. I like to think that I discovered value in Coke before Warren Buffett. The rest is history. As you can imagine, we hit pay dirt, the mother lode, the big tamale, the whole enchilada. You get the idea. The only thing we did wrong was—you guessed it—we sold much too soon.

Coca-Cola 1980–1990

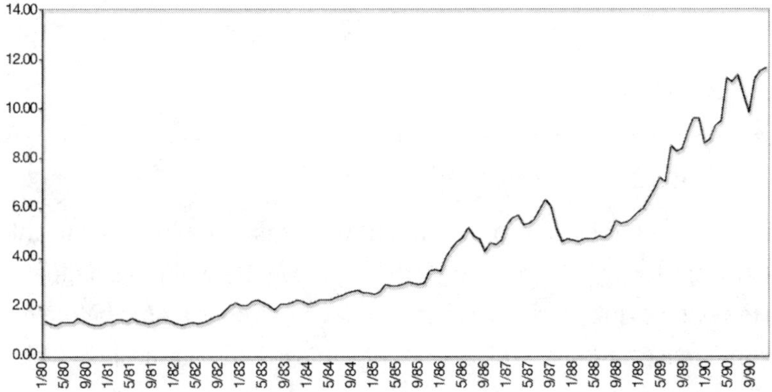

PepsiCo 1980–1990

McDonald's 1980–1990

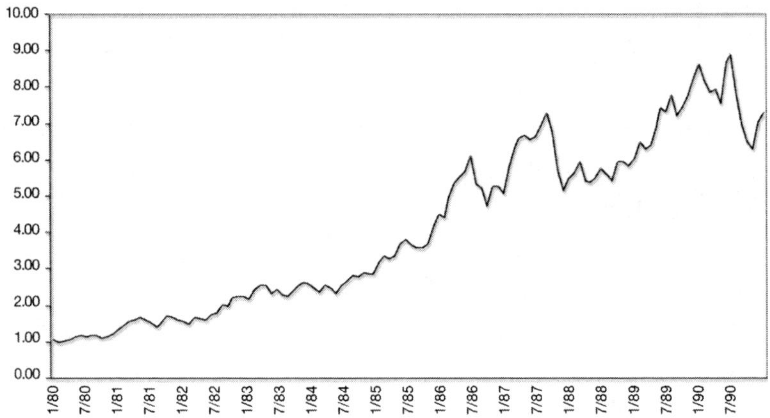

Just the other day an accountant was telling me how he bought Certicom below $5, before it started to move. How did this happen? He's out looking for rental space and one location is rented before he could make an offer, so he asks, "Who's moving in?" "Certicom, a high-tech company downstairs, is expanding," was the response. He checks out the company, called his broker and the rest is history: $5 to eventually $250 and then back to below $50. A great pass, as they say in the business, but also he sells too soon.

It should also be of interest that in each case, all of these investors sold too early. This is hard not to do and puts them in good company.

Certicom 1999–2000

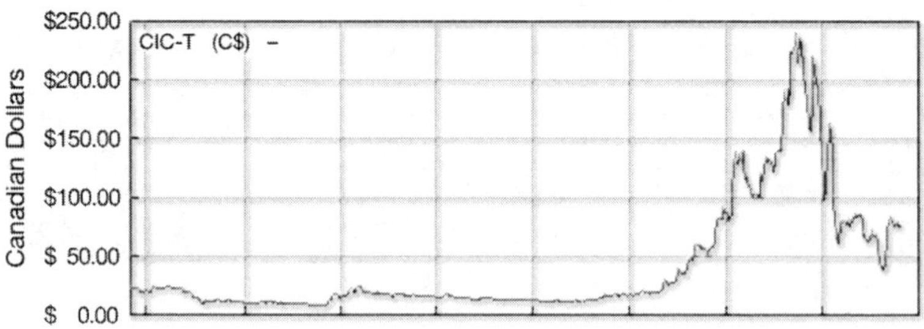

www.certicom.com

"I got wealthy by selling too soon."
John D. Rockefeller

Did you know that John D. Rockefeller, born July 8, 1839, became the founder of Standard Oil and at one time accounted for over three-quarters of all the oil production in the United States? This was before the U.S. Supreme Court broke up the company in 1911 into 38 separate companies that comprised the Standard Oil Company. These are the same Sherman antitrust laws that Bill Gates and Microsoft are fighting today. The United States has a long history of fighting monopolies and preserving competition.

The world has no shortage of ideas. They're right in front of you, day in and day out. You just have to be attuned to the signs of an opportunity. However, if you are really true to this approach, it's unlikely that you will uncover more than four or five opportunities a year and you'll be lucky if two of those jump out at you as being irresistible. Be like Warren Buffett: wait for the right pitch. Keep in mind that we are looking for situations that can yield 50% to 300% and more.

The one thing that is not generally known is that most people who make a lot of money, do it on relatively few stock positions in their lifetimes. Bill Gates of Microsoft or Larry Ellison of Oracle hold stocks in which they have large positions that double, triple, quadruple or more. Since you now realize how seldom great opportunities such as these come along, it shouldn't surprise you that most of the wealthy traders I know have made vastly disproportionate contributions to their net worth over the course of their careers from one or two such well-researched opportunities, such as Fairfax Financial, Aber Resources, Polysar, Virtek Vision, Nortel, Microsoft and Chrysler.

One book that's as helpful as it is enlightening about discovering and acting on those special opportunities is Peter Lynch's book *One Up on Wall Street,* which I recommend as a primer for those who wish to trade individual stocks.

Exceptional opportunities come along only rarely. But, every so often you are confronted with an opportunity that, right from the start, you know is going nowhere. Often the best test of an investment is your nose; check to see if the deal smells. In 1995, my family and I spent a week at a dude ranch in Tucson, Arizona, the Lazy K Bar Ranch. I'm out at the corral, when Wrangler Bob saunters over for a conversation, which starts with horses, drifts to cows, to UFOs, then women and finally investments, a topic I know something about. Wrangler Bob is doing all the talking; I'm doing all the listening. It's not long before I have a good idea of his net worth—a saddle that his grandfather left him that's seen better days, and a 12-year-old pickup truck that's been, as they say, driven hard and put away wet. All in, I'd say U.S.$1,800, tops. He leans over and says:

"So, you're in the investment game."

"Yep," I reply (I'm trying to get into character).

"I have been working on an idea for some time, I just need some capital. Wait here. I have an offering memorandum in the pickup," he says.

Offering memorandum in the pickup truck! I was about to run then, but curiosity froze me to the bench. He's back in no time.

"I have the working plans to a perpetual motion machine," he whispers.

"Sorry, Wrangler Bob, that's my daughter calling."

Sometimes the best defense against a bad investment is simply to walk away, and like most investors I can think of more than a few situations that I wish I had just walked away from.

And then there are those opportunities lost. Sometimes, opportunities present themselves—the reasoning is right and everything comes together. But for some unknown reason, you fail to act—fail to take advantage of the opportunity. It's unexplainable. This includes me, and years later it still annoys me.

Chrysler 1980–1998

In 1984, I'm looking at Chrysler. The stock is $3 and everyone thinks it's going broke. I am out for a long jog and am remembering what Kenneth Galbraith has said about very large companies in America having no entrepreneurial risk. Because of their largeness, no government will let them fail because of the huge negative effect on the economy as a whole and I'm also thinking about Lee Iacocca, the guy who gave us the Mustang. But for some reason, I just never got around to following through.

There was another big missed opportunity the previous year. The bellwether Canadian bond was the 9-1/2 s of 01. They traded close to 50 cents on the dollar for a yield of 18%. I'm trading them for about a quarter of my clients. I have always sincerely believed that by the time a problem, as serious as inflation was in the early 1980s, is well recognized, all the processes to solve it are mobilized. Next year, they redeem at par from 1983 to 2001, a guaranteed yield of 18% assuming that the government of Canada can stay solvent until 2001 to pay off the yield and principal. Again, for some reason, I just never got around to this either.

During the 1970s, while teaching college, I did some archaeological research in the summer, and we were camped out on Somerset Island, just a couple of air hours south of Resolute, Northwest Territories.

9 1/2 2001 Government of Canada 1980–1990

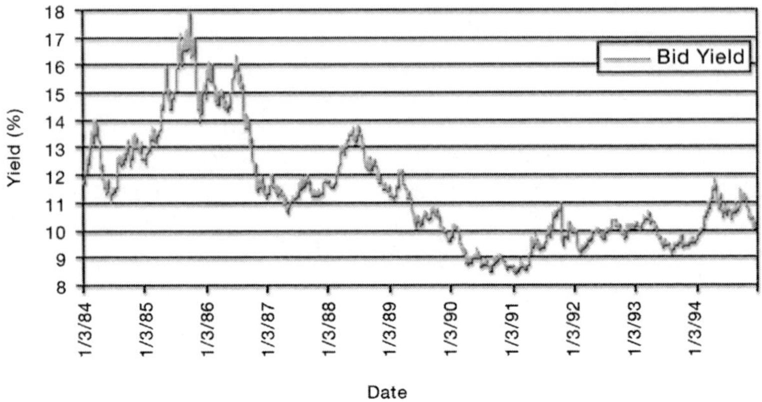

Our camp was visited by a geologist from the Geological Survey of Canada—Kerr, I believe his name was. Anyway, he has a Bell 47 helicopter, just like the ones in *M.A.S.H.* We got to know each other and I relate to him my interest in fossil hunting.

Bell produced a total of 6,263 of these helicopters before ending production in 1973. The company is named after Lawrence J. Bell, was started on July 10, 1935, and delivered its first Bell 47, the helicopter made famous by *M.A.S.H.*, on December 30, 1946.

The next thing I know, we're off. He's looking for rock samples and directing me to fossil deposits. During the day, our conversation wanders over a number of subjects, but the one I remember most relates to diamonds.

"There are diamonds up here," he says. "Very similar deposits, formations to those in South Africa, kimberlitic pipes." I am still thinking fossils.

"They would just be industrial-grade stuff, wouldn't they?" I ask.

"Never know, the formations are very similar."

He finds a neat rock and I find a neat fossil and diamonds never come up again.

In 1992, when I was working for Richardson Greenshields, diamonds come up again—Diamet and then Aber Resources—and there's ongoing discussions as to whether Canada's Northwest Territories has diamonds. After all, diamonds only come from warm climates such as South Africa, not Northwest Territories, Canada. But I know different. Diamet pops first. Then Aber Resources is in the fray with lots of time to buy at $1 before it eventually goes to $28. I had a friend who's into it in a big way but for some reason, I just never got around to it.

Aber Resources

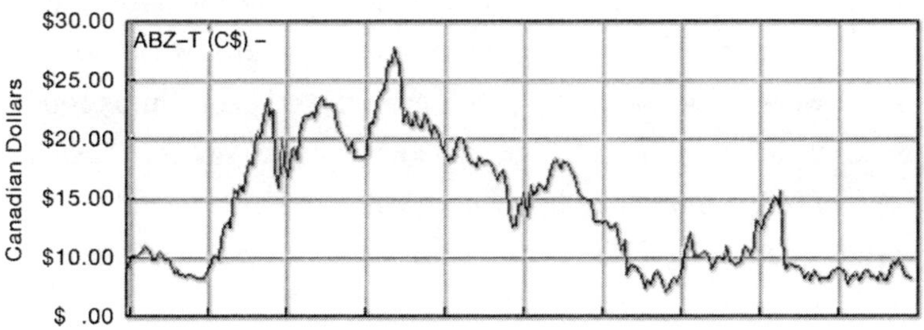

www.aber.ca/index1.htm

RULE #3. You will not trade that often, and you will research many stocks before you are satisfied that you have just the opportunity you want under the circumstances and conditions that afford you the highest probability of success. But when such opportunities do present themselves, seize the moment.

When it comes to execution—that is, *how to trade*—I would be remiss if I did not begin by directing you to two books about Jesse Livermore, perhaps the greatest Wall Street trader of all time. What Robert Johnson is to rock and roll, Jesse Livermore is to trading. Don't make another trade before you read these books. Both were written in the 1920s and they're timeless.

Jesse Livermore, Speculator King, by Paul Sarnoff, is a fascinating biography of the most revered market speculator of all time, who was blamed for causing the crash of 1929 and credited with calling every market correction from 1917 to 1940. This book is a must-read for all investors.

Reminiscences of a Stock Operator, by Edwin Lefevre, was published in 1923 and is considered to be the quintessential text on the market and trading. You can spend U.S.$18.95 and a few hours to carefully read this, or you can waste untold dollars and years and, perhaps, still not learn what this text has to offer. The choice is yours.

To start with, we must get you in the right philosophical space to position yourself for successful trading. Think of being in the market as comparable to bull riding: you have no control over the bull, except when to get on and off, and even the off part can be rough. (Ask anyone who's had a margin call.) For those of you that have not experienced a margin call, when you buy a stock on margin you borrow against the value of the stock based on a percentage of its value. If you are fully margined (that is, at the limit of this allowable percentage as many investors are) and the stock goes down, the allowable margin value decreases and you must either put in more money or sell the stock. Most people buy on margin because they do not have cash, so when a margin call comes they must sell, which further accelerates the downward movement of the stock, prompting further margin calls and worsening the situation. Understand from the outset that you have no control of the market and, just as in bull riding, your ability to predict its movements is limited at best. But at least with bull riding, it's all over in eight seconds.

Unlike bull riding, where you don't get to choose the bull, in the market, you at least get to pick the stock. So now that you've chosen the stock, all your efforts must be directed at two elements you have control over: when to buy the stock and when to sell it. Of the two decisions, when to get off, or sell, is the one that defines the quintessential trader. Just like bull riding, if it's a bad ride, you must get off with as little damage to yourself as possible. For us, as investors, that means protecting capital. We can ride again if our capital remains intact. If not, we are out of business. On the bright side, unlike bull riding, once you get off a bad stock trade, the pain is over. It doesn't then turn around and try to kill you.

> "A loss never bothers me after I take it. I forget it overnight. But being wrong—not taking the loss—that is what does damage to the pocket-book and the soul."
>
> *Jesse Livermore*

Capital Protection

What is not widely understood is that a professional trader is not necessarily successful because he or she chooses more stocks that go up than down, but because when he or she takes a loss, it is small, and when he or she takes a profit, it is large. In fact, it is not uncommon for a successful trader to have two or more losing trades for each profitable one. Now, since we're taking few but relatively large positions, and as a percentage of the entire investment they account for 5% to 20%, you must monitor these positions and periodically reevaluate them by updating the research sheet. Diversification is accomplished through the 75% portfolio segment, while stock trading is highly concentrated to generate large gains. Here, gains of 50% and greater would be the norm. Preservation of capital is still paramount, but within the trading strategy it is accomplished not by diversification but by selling the position quickly if it moves against you.

Keep in mind that there are two elements to wealth: making it and keeping it. There are far fewer of those who keep it than those who make it. Capital protection is misunderstood and underrated, but suffice it to say that if you're out of capital, you're out of the game.

"I made enough money to buy Miami
but it wasn't meant to last."
Jimmy Buffett

It's the late 1980s. A friend approaches me about what to do with the money from the sale of his company, which is well into the seven-figure range. Whether this is a lot of money depends on whom you hang around with.

"What should I do?" he asks.

"Let's put it in perspective," I suggest. "It's not enough money to buy your own jet or own a place in Florida and the south of France, but if you are careful it's certainly enough to rent a place in Florida and the south of France and fly business-class whenever you want."

I continue: "There isn't an appreciable lifestyle difference between someone with say $5 million and $15 million, but there is a big difference in lifestyles between someone with $0 and $5 million. And there is no legitimate argument for risking the capital."

He's thinking, if I lever up this money I can reach the $20 million level, soon, maybe very soon.

"Keep in mind that someone with this amount of capital properly invested with some patience will eventually have $10 million to $20 million anyway. It just takes time and a proper investment portfolio," I say.

In fact, in the August 8, 2000, edition of *The Financial Post,* Germain Lamonde, Exfo's founder and one of Canada's newest high-tech multibillionaires, says, "Once you have about $20 million, you've got more than you'll ever need," and this would be in today's money.

At moments like this I often think back to my high school days at Queen Elizabeth Collegiate and Vocational Institute, in Kingston, Ontario, and in particular to my Grade 12 class picture. I ask myself, how am I doing compared to the other guys? It was an all-boys class. I find this to be a most sobering and steadying reflection that one can bring to bear when contemplating the risk of capital. This image in my mind

is an anchor fixed firmly in reality, a point from which to measure life's successes and failures. For me, this 40-year-old black-and-white image has always been a way to put important things in perspective.

Call it greed, call it hubris, call it being an entrepreneur, but my friend exposed all the capital to a single real estate venture and lost, and has started over again. He's on his way to doing well again, but it's the "again" part that could have been avoided. The capital protection issue is not treated with the respect it deserves. It's also about compounding. Doesn't anyone understand compounding?

Rule #4. You must always protect capital by being willing to cut short losses and not being too anxious to take a profit and thus cut profits short.

Before we go further, let's forget about trying to sell at the top and buy at the bottom. Keep in mind that there are more Panda bears in the world than there are people who buy at the bottom and sell at the top. The good thing about Panda bears is they don't go to dinner parties and brag to everyone about market-timing.

And let's kill one more dangerous misconception, the value of inside information in the stock-selection process.

"With enough inside information and a million dollars, you can go broke in a year."
Warren Buffett

Did you know that Warren Buffett and Jimmy Buffett aren't related, but they are both doing well? Warren is one of the wealthiest men in America and Jimmy is one of the highest-paid performers in America.

In the universe, the speed of light is the great constant, whereas in investing, the market itself is the great constant. If you do two years of research on a stock and after you buy the stock it goes down, you're wrong because, by definition, the market is always right. There can be no discussion on the point. If you take time to discuss it or justify it or rationalize it, then you have broken Rule #4 and exposed yourself to greater capital loss.

Cognitive Dissonance

The great bogeyman of human nature is "cognitive dissonance." You're in high school and you can't decide whether to take Peggy-Sue or Mary-Lou to the dance. They both have charming but different attributes and different but unpleasant warts. You finally decide on Peggy-Sue because Ricky Nelson has already asked Mary-Lou. As soon as you decide, however, your mind starts to rewrite history. It unknowingly begins to emphasize all of Peggy-Sue's attributes and Mary-Lou's warts, thus making your decision seem all the more correct. This is no big deal when all that is at stake is a $5 corsage and half a tube of Brillcreme, but when it's the market, and it's your hard-earned after-tax cash, it's a different story.

So you do the research, you buy a stock, and it immediately goes down; and in kicks that bogeyman, cognitive dissonance. "I was early. No problem. I'll simply buy more." "Gosh, at this price, it's an even better bargain. I'll buy more." "I can't believe my good luck. No one else can see the opportunity. I'll buy more." Or my personal favorite:

"If I buy more now, I can average down my price and the stock doesn't have to go up as much for me to get my money back." Each of these reactions is an insidious attempt by your mind to rewrite history and make your initial decision look as if it was correct when, in fact, it wasn't. As my teenage daughter would say, "Looooser." You're going downtown and you accidentally got on a bus going to the suburbs. Get off the bus. Sell the stock now. Control your losses. Protect your capital and never average down. Remember Rule #4.

> "Markets are never wrong, opinions are. ... There is only one side of the market and it is not the bull side or the bear side. It is the right side."
>
> *Jesse Livermore*

You buy a stock and it starts to go up. But you can't bring yourself to buy more. Now averaging up, buying more stock as the price increases, is the other story and again, the old bogeyman, cognitive dissonance, is playing devil's advocate with your mind. "Who would pay these prices? I couldn't buy here." "I always buy at the bottom. I can't buy now." "Good thing I got it when the price was reasonable. It's too expensive to buy now." And again my favorite: "I should have bought more." You were willing to add to your position when the price was going to hell in a handbasket, but you are not willing when the price is climbing up like a homesick angel. You freeze. My daughter's word rings in my ears again, "Looooser."

Rule #5. The market is always right. Never average down, only up. And if you're tempted to resort to prayer, it's time to get out.

Selling is straightforward. When you buy, you set a target, not afterwards, but when you buy. And when the stock hits the target, you quickly review the stock-selection sheet to see whether there is any compelling reason why the target should be changed or raised. If not, you sell the whole position. If a stock is rising in price on heavy volume or increasing volume, it's worth looking at redoing the stock-selection sheet and potentially raising the sell target price. The review is necessary because you must let the profits run.

Remember that a professional is likely to have two to three losing trades for every one that's profitable, so the profitable ones must be significantly greater than the losing ones. Your losses on the losers should be significantly smaller than your gains on the profitable ones. In the brokerage business, this is known as weeding the garden, pulling the bad stocks out of your portfolio, letting the good stocks have room to grow.

RULE #6. Sell a stock—all of the stock—when it reaches the price target you set when you bought it, unless a complete review of the stock-selection sheet convinces you to raise the target price.

An amateur investor will often refuse to sell a stock when it goes down because "it owes him or her money" and to take a loss is to admit that he or she has made a mistake. On the other hand, many investors are too anxious to take a profit because taking a profit makes them right. This seemingly reasonable but insidious methodology is disastrous. Over time, it means that you are constantly selling the good stocks and keeping the dogs. Remember, you're not in the kennel business; you're in the business of making money.

The other option is that the stock hasn't performed. If it hasn't gone up or down, review the stock-selection sheet and treat it like a new position. If it still meets the criteria, hold. If it fails, sell and look for another opportunity. Patience is often required. In fact, it often takes longer than you had anticipated. Successful investors may hold a stock for years. Keep in mind that the average value manager holds a stock for about three years. Remember, a stock can't tell time. It doesn't know you're in a hurry. It doesn't care about your costs of carrying the investment, or the fact that your mortgage payment is coming due. A stock is just one of thousands of soulless players in a godless market. It can bestow good fortune on bad people, and misfortune on good people. Regardless, you must not sell too soon or set too low a target.

> "I wish that I knew what I know now, when I was younger."
>
> *Rod Stewart*

Summary

RULE #1. Trading is not a game. It's a business and, as such, you should only be actively in business when the conditions greatly favor your success.

RULE #2. Trading is an activity done in concert with your whole portfolio and should be restricted to a portion no greater than 25% of the whole.

RULE #3. You will not trade that often, and you will research many stocks before you are satisfied that you have just the opportunity you want under the circumstances and conditions that afford you the highest probability of success. But when such opportunities do present themselves, seize the moment.

RULE #4. You must always protect capital by being willing to cut short losses and not being too anxious to take a profit and thus cut profits short.

RULE #5. The market is always right. Never average down, only up. And if you're tempted to resort to prayer, it's time to get out.

RULE #6. Sell a stock—all of the stock—when it reaches the price target you set when you bought it, unless a complete review of the stock-selection sheet convinces you to raise the target price.

If, after this, you're convinced that you still wish to trade individual stocks for your own account (we hope in association with a properly constructed Opus 2 portfolio constituting of at least 75% of your invested wealth), you've memorized the six rules of investing and you promise yourself that you will behave yourself, then there is one other item that you should own: *The Stock Trader's Almanac.* It's a great store of market superstitions, trivia and folklore and makes for a fascinating read. It's available from The Hirsch Organization at www.stocktradersalmanac.com. It really should be part of your trading kit along with that HP 17B calculator.

Day Trading

With all the hype and press about day trading I feel compelled to mention that what we have so carefully outlined over the last chapter is not day trading, nor are we advocating such.

"My neighbor across the street is a day trader," a friend says. "She's set up in the basement and she trades every day. I am thinking of doing the same thing with some savings I have put aside." This was in March; the timing couldn't have been worse.

> "The minute it looks like money, everyone wants in."
> *Frank Zappa*

Day trading is virtually a form of gambling, meaning most traders lose money but the brokerage firm (house) profits from the commissions generated on each and every trade. At least 90% of all day traders lose money and at least 60% lose *all* their money because they're untrained and up against professionals with a lot more timely information, more savvy and much deeper pockets.

Day trading is a bit misleading. The average losing trade is held about 9.53 days and the average winning trade about 4.52 days, which suggests that these trades are cutting short profits and letting their losses run. Yet, the most alarming research shows that the average trader was risking 100% of capital on each trade and that there was extensive use of borrowed money (margin).

NASDAQ Spring of 2000

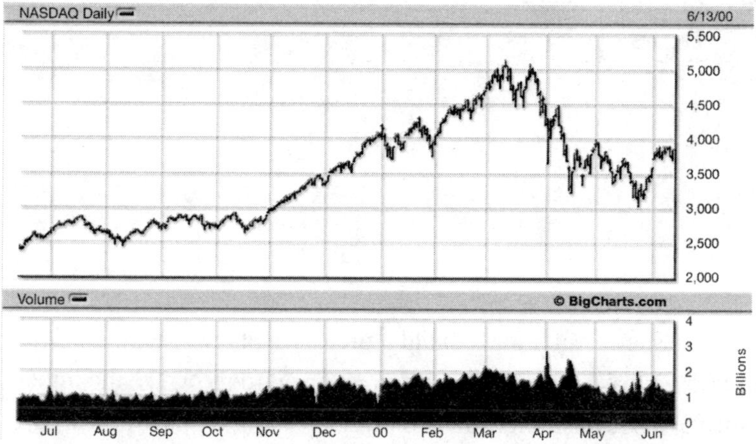

www.BigCharts.com

Day trading or short-term trading has the look and feel of the South Sea Bubble of 1711 or the Tulip Mania of 1636. It is not investing. It has no defensible role in wealth creation, which is precisely why I mention it. Remember, we must remain focused on wealth creation.

As a point of encouragement, there is one powerful underlying force that favors your venture. Wealth is *created* in the stock markets. Granted, wealth is also transferred, but the key underlying precept of the markets is that they actually create wealth. This is unlike, say, the commodity market, a zero-sum game that can only transfer wealth; in this market for one person to profit, someone has to lose. That's not the case with equity markets. Equity markets over the long term create wealth for the majority of those involved. In the equity market, everyone can profit, simply by being a long-term portfolio investor. Keep one more thing in mind before you become a trader and push your hard-earned, after-tax cash out onto the stock-trading floor:

> "If you don't know who you are,
> the stock market is an expensive place to find out."
>
> *George Goodman*

Conclusion "Pearls"

We have shown you how to build a professional investment portfolio. In fact, we have practically pleaded with you to recognize the importance of asset-class selection and diversification. We have also argued for active professional money managers and the necessity of patience and staying the course. And we've gone out of our way to show you the dangers and pitfalls of straying from the reasonable course.

We recognize that you're only human and that temptations of greed are always there, tempting you away from this proven course to trading stocks for the big score. Should the lure of easy money be too tempting and your will too weak, we have even gone so far as to instruct you in the art of trading individual stocks, showing you how to limit your risk and maximize your returns by selecting and trading a few good stock positions in relationship to that core investment portfolio.

Along the way, I also shared some of my adventures and misadventures in the investment market, but my experiences represent only a small cross section of what the market has to offer. Many of my friends and colleagues have similar experiences, victories and setbacks from which we could all benefit. I was fortunate to have been given good advice at the right time, and it has made all the difference.

In my third year with McLeod, I made the chairman's list of top producers and was invited to a black-tie affair in Toronto. Big deal for me, old hat for others. We're in the King Edward Hotel. All the top guys and gals are there. I am feeling bulletproof. At the event, Austin Taylor approaches me. I'm a bit surprised and nervous—not only is he the chairman, but he's also a legend. We shake hands, my hand disappears into his; he's six feet five inches, 350 pounds. "Allen," he said, "you're doing quite well in Ottawa."

"Thank you, Mr. Taylor." Accepting a compliment is always a pleasant task. He's breathing heavily and looking straight at me, and I realize that this is no chance meeting. He has an agenda.

"You wouldn't be spending all that money you're making, now would you, Allen?" he says. "No, Mr. Taylor," was all I could say before he continued: "You're putting some aside. Good." And he moved off into the crowd.

Short and sweet, deliberate, right on the money, the right words at the right time, and better advice than "Plastics."

If I could translate this into advice for others, it is to live below your means. Only then will you have a surplus to invest, and only then can you begin wealth creation. It's all about Opus 2, the second work, when you make available a portion of your earnings so that your money can work for you as opposed to you only working for money.

Following are a set of priceless experiences related to me for our benefit from an eclectic group of professional investors, mostly Canadians, who average more than 20 years of experience in the investment or related industry, and who over the years have done well but not without the occasional setback.

However, you can bet that these successful investors don't make the same mistakes twice, but in pushing the investment envelope forward, they are likely to encounter completely new experiences—some good, some bad. I think you will find these experiences helpful, particularly if you try to identify patterns as to why they were successful and why they weren't, and then apply the advice to your own investment activities.

"Those who cannot remember the past
are condemned to repeat it."
Santayana

Fairfax Financial Holdings Jan. 01 1996–Jan. 01 2000

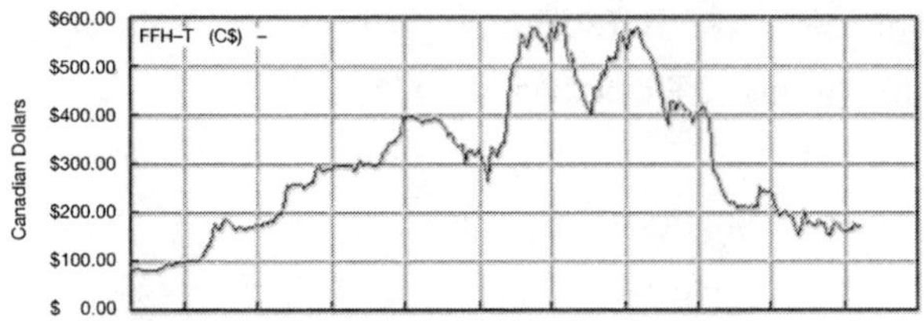

www.globeinvestor.com

JOHN SMITH, Director, Scotia McLeod

Thirty-plus years' experience, no two alike. Started in the brokerage business in 1969.

ADVICE: "Invest in good companies with excellent management and good track records, where management has a significant financial stake in the success of the company, and hold the investment as long as the above conditions are in place."

BEST INVESTMENT: "Fairfax Financial. I paid $18.00 a share in 1991. The stock is currently $175.00 per share. Book value has grown from $2.08 in 1985 to $231.00 in 1999. Prem Watsa, the CEO, has substantially all his personal net worth in Fairfax shares (the stock has been as high as $604.00)."

WORST INVESTMENT: "Speculations, particularly junior oils and junior mines; Sikamin Mines comes to mind. The number of juniors that actually become companies are extremely rare. In 30 years I am probably even, but what a waste of time and energy."

BILL ASHBY, President, Beutel Goodman

Thirty-five years' experience in the pension investment area. Always on the value side; never loses the faith, never strays, a true believer.

ADVICE: "Always remember there is a difference between a great investment and a great company. A company may be superb on the basis of its fundamentals, strong experienced management, high growth rates and high profitability. However, even a great company can be a speculative investment if the price paid to participate as an investor is excessive given the company's historical experience and longer-term potential. Price is a critical component of any sound investment decision."

Stelco Jan. 01 1996–Jan. 01 2000

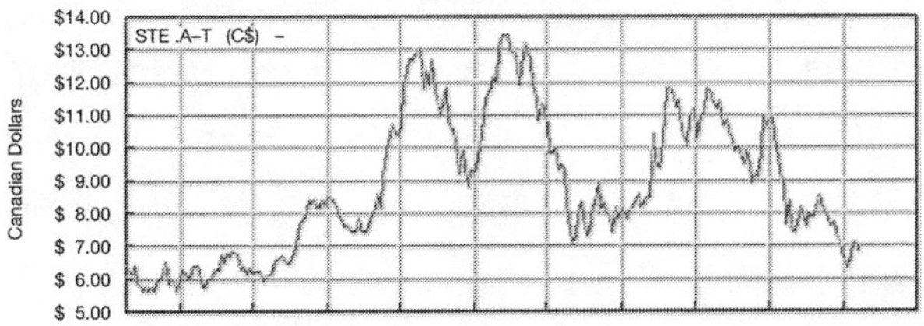

www.globeinvestor.com

Best Investment: "In 1992, Stelco had declined from a high $10.00 to 90 cents in response to investor concerns driven by U.S. accusations of unfair trade practices. It was my impression that while the United States might prove unfair practices it would not be possible to prove injury due to very buoyant steel markets. This proved to be the case and the stock subsequently recovered to its previous high of $10.00 in 1993."

Worst Investment: "My purchase of a small, unproven concept company by the name of Punter Graphics. The stock rose from 50 cents to $5.00 strictly on the basis of promotion and unrealistic expectations for future profits. The company ultimately declared bankruptcy. The moral: investigate before you invest and beware of highly promoted concept stocks."

JOHN MCDONALD, Chairman and CEO, McDonald Financial Corporation
Former analyst at the International Monetary Fund and one of the best foreign equity managers in the country.

Advice: "Risk simply comes from not knowing what you are doing. Manage your risk by investing in what you know. If you don't know, find someone who does."

Best Investment: "Buying my own funds."

Worst Investment: "In the early 1980s, IBM July 140 call options, a large position on which I stubbornly averaged down from December through April. The stock soared through 140 in August and I used the tax losses the following year. Being right is not enough. Never fight the tape, the Fed or the clock."

FRED KETCHUM, Managing Director, Scotia McLeod

Thirty-plus years' experience. Considered by most as one of the most experienced equity traders in Canada; regardless of market gyrations, he is always unflappable.

Advice: "Do your own homework and invest for the long term—that's at least a two-year period."

Best Investment: "Bank of Nova Scotia, from $6.75 in 1988 to $37 today plus all the dividends. Acquired it first on the BNS takeout of McLeod Young Weir and added to the position a number of times since. Did very well on Bombardier also."

Worst Investment: "AMNEX Inc. on the NASDAQ. They were in the pay-telephone business just before cell phones took off. I paid $4, got caught up in the story, relied on someone else for information and didn't do my own research. It is now worth 5 cents—wrong time, wrong place, and wrong stock. Should have bought Nokia."

> "If I had my life to live over again, I would elect to be a trader of goods rather than a student of science."
>
> *Albert Einstein*

GEORGE ANDERSON, President and CEO, Insurance Bureau of Canada

Former president of Canada Mortgage and Housing Corporation, always wanted to be a trader.

Advice: "No matter how successful you become, do not confuse your bank account with your IQ. The market is smarter than the players in it in the long run. No investor is right 100% of the time and those who forget the underlying fundamentals of what constitutes value in companies will be wrong for their clients more often than they will be right."

Best Investment: "When I became a partner and director of the St. Catharines Stompers, the Class A franchise of the Toronto Blue Jays. Apart from the economic value of the investment, there was an opportunity to be part of a business where the product was good family entertainment. Anytime you become involved in doing something you really enjoy and make a little profit too, that's a good investment in my books."

WORST INVESTMENT: "Be very wary of family-owned businesses, especially where succession is uncertain. I am not talking primarily of large, long-established corporations but rather of small and medium-sized companies where the personality of the founder plays a large role in creating confidence in the firm. In addition to the normal problems of business, these enterprises can be subject to internal power struggles exacerbated by private family issues or poor leadership when the patriarch prefers family members to professional management."

"Financial genius is a rising stock market."
Kenneth Galbraith

JAMES KERMES, President and CEO, Glenmede Trust Company
More than 30 years' investment experience with high-net-worth clients.
www.glenmede.com

ADVICE: "Investors tend to overcomplicate investment decisions and be too short-term oriented. Be a long-term investor and focus on two things: earnings and management. Focus on these and control your emotions. Financial markets are simply statistical reflections of human emotion, swinging like an erratic pendulum between fear and greed. Successful long-term investors capitalize on the extremes."

BEST INVESTMENT: "My career in the investment business—it is constantly exciting and stimulating."

WORST INVESTMENT: "The worst investment I ever made was more of a mental nightmare than a financial one. It was in a limited partnership of land investments. I ignored the quality of management. The land was sound, but the general partner turned out to be a crook. I was lucky and escaped financially whole due to one of the most street-savvy lawyers I have ever known."

BRIAN COSTELLO, one of Canada's best-known commentators, authors and seminar speakers on personal finance
The man who for 30 years has been "taking care of yourrrr money."

Advice: "A multidimensional approach has been a win-win strategy for me. Core holdings should be proven investments that have been there and will be there in all times and in all markets. Ford is a prime example. Someday, cars may run without tires or even gasoline. But you can bet your last dollar that Ford will be there assembling them. Banks fit into the same mold. They're solid dividend payers and a significant growth opportunity in markets around the world as a result of the diversification that is transforming the financial services industry in recent years."

Best Investment: "That's easy: Alcan. First purchased when I was six and sold many times and repurchased many times and still owned, producing tremendous returns over the years. It's a classic multidimensional investment—one that's always going to be there, pays a dividend in U.S. funds and continues to grow its business and its profits."

Worst Investment: "It was in a company started by one of my friends. That was my first mistake. The company was not publicly traded and my investment had no liquidity. That was my second. And every time I asked for a report on how the company was doing, I was assured everything was fine and proceeding on schedule. That was my third mistake. I later learned this was not the case. It also reaffirmed the importance of multidimensional investing, including liquidity and the critical issue of corporate reporting and timely disclosure."

GREG GUICHON, Investment Executive and Director, Scotia McLeod

Never satisfied with last year's performance, constantly seeking innovation to get results.

Advice: "Good companies get better and bad companies just get worse, so be sure to cut your losses short. You are always going to make bad investments; it's realizing it and doing something about it quickly that makes the difference."

Best Investment: "Fairfax Financial: bought it at $28, sold above $400. A prime example of a good company that just gets better."

Worst Investment: "They were too many to name just one."

"Success is going from failure to failure without loss of enthusiasm."
Sir Winston Churchill

GEDD CANTWELL started in 1981 selling MURBs and then went to Merrill Lynch in Eastern Canada, before ending up on the Prairies with Rampart Securities

Gedd just couldn't stop at one piece of advice—he has one for the fixed-income market and one for the equity markets.

ADVICE: "Never chase yield; there is always a reason for the extraordinary rate the company is paying. Find out why, and always buy the horse, not the cart. Bells and whistles make a cart look pretty, but the horse is what makes it move." After 25 years as a broker Gedd added that, no matter what, all winning trades were the client's ideas, and all losing trades were the broker's ideas.

BEST INVESTMENT: "I would have to say a company called Net Shepherd at a very early stage and working with management to put in a solid team to build the company. It has been a long road with many twists and turns, but rewarding and fruitful."

WORST INVESTMENT: "Not buying more of my previously mentioned pick, Net Shepherd."

TOM KIERANS, Chairman, Moore Corp.; board member, Petro-Canada; Chairman and CEO, Canadian Institute of Advanced Research

Former president of McLeod Young and Weir, former president and CEO of the C. D. Howe Institute, former chairman of Petro-Canada. Few people in Canada have a better understanding of capital markets and what drives them.

ADVICE: "Berard Baruch said it best and for all time: 'Investigate the fundamentals, invest on the basis of the fundamentals and hold, transaction costs are prohibitive.'"

BEST INVESTMENT: "My best investment came to me on the sale of my McLeod Young and Weir share in return for the Bank of Nova Scotia shares. I knew the senior executive and I understood the fundamentals of the operation and its strategic direction. I held, and tax considerations did not enter the picture."

Worst Investment: "The period 1980–85 was dominated in Canada by devaluation, a faith in commodity price increases, excessive government intervention and poor fundamentals. In a herd mentality, I lost a bundle—and on margin. Get the fundamentals right and forgo leverage in the equity markets."

RICK HESSION, Entrepreneur and Restaurateur

Former owner of six McDonald's restaurants. Presently operates Cache Cache Bistro, one of the finest eateries in Aspen, Colorado.

Advice: "If I could advise my 14-year-old daughter Danielle in a few words about where to spend her money and time, they would be: broadband wireless. Thirty years ago it would have been plastics."

Best Investment: "Many years ago, my friend and adviser, Bob Armstrong, suggested that I purchase 'a couple of shares of Berkshire Hathaway' so that I could receive the Berkshire Annual Report from the brilliant Warren Buffett. Berkshire Hathaway was then at $400 per share. Wisely, I acted immediately on his advice. As I write, these shares are at $53,800 and have been as high as $80,000."

Worst Investment: "I took Bob's advice literally and bought two shares. You can do the math. If I had purchased only 100 shares for $40,000, I would now have a portfolio in Berkshire alone of $5,380,000."

GLEN MOORE started with McLeod Young and Weir in 1964

Thirty-six years' experience; never a day when he wasn't excited to come to work.

Advice: "It is vitally important today for investors and their advisers to understand goals and objectives for long-term investing. If the individual investor is interested in building and retaining wealth and/or passing on wealth to the next generation, a comprehensive investment program is a necessity. Start with an investment portfolio."

Best Investment: "The best investment I have made has been to implement a fully diversified asset-allocation program, a true investment portfolio for my core investments, that allows for maximum return for the minimum amount of risk."

WORST INVESTMENT: "My worst investment has been overconcentration in one stock or sector that I knew little about. In 1988 I made an investment in cattle—livestock. It was something I knew about; it was high return, high risk, motivated by greed. Greed lost, as it often does."

JIM MUIR, Head of Research, Canaccord

More than 30 years in the investment industry. One of the early Quant researchers and an early believer in the Canadian diamond industry.

ADVICE: "I remain a believer in investing in individual companies. Pay attention to the management, because no matter how good the investment looks it all comes down to management and their ability to execute."

BEST INVESTMENT: "I bought flow-through shares of a small oil company, Belator Explorations. I researched the situation carefully and liked the management, because they were able to execute the plan, I stayed with it and the stock rose 25-fold before I sold."

WORST INVESTMENT: "A concept stock, Ecoval, based on organic herbicides and natural fertilizers, but the management just wasn't capable of executing the plan."

JIM WILHELM, a broker with Merrill Lynch

He started in 1980 with Goulding, Rose and Turner, one of the real survivors in the industry; always puts the client first.

ADVICE: "Never buy a stock on the talk of a takeover. In the past 20 years I have heard of hundreds of takeovers and rarely if ever does the takeover happen. When they do, they always happen out of the blue without any warning."

BEST INVESTMENT: "Buying into a private equity deal that owned some shares in a high-tech company called Ditech. The company went public at $12 a share and moved up to $260 a share within a year."

WORST INVESTMENT: "Selling Ditech way too soon. Also shorting Nortel in October 1999 and being stupid enough to hold the short—all the way to the top of the market."

DAVID PATTERSON, President, Newcastle Capital Management Inc. Credited by many with starting the RSP-eligible products in Canada, considered one of the leading derivative experts in Canada and a governor of the Montreal Exchange.

Advice: "For the small investor, the most profitable assumption to make is that markets are efficient. This means that, over the long run, active management doesn't outperform the index—certainly not after the extra costs associated with active management. Believing that some 'superior' managers outperform the index leads to a constant chase after the 'hot' manager. This chase only adds the variability of manager's results to the variability of the stock and bond markets. So, for optimal long-term performance, my solution is to index all the major markets of the globe.

"For institutional investors, there are ways to access niche inefficiencies in markets and add these returns to the index returns. Still, the base of any portfolio should be index funds."

Best Investment: "Eleven years ago, I had the opportunity to establish Newcastle Capital Management and to invest in a stellar group of people. Without a doubt, the decision to invest in the firm and its people has proven to be the best investment I ever made."

Worst Investment: "Several years back, I invested in three tax partnerships. They all turned out to be dogs. Since then, I have had a rule that has greatly simplified my life: it is better to pay tax to the government than to pay tax to promoters, tax lawyers and accountants. At least then you receive some benefit."

Chart of Cisco Sept.1998–Sept. 2000

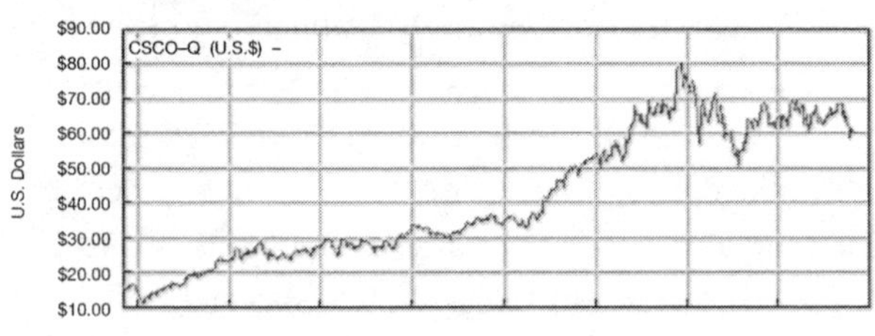

www.globleinvestor.com

SONNY STANIFORD, 25-plus years' investment experience; trader on the floor of the New York Stock Exchange with Pershing for 20 years In the market when the Dow was below 500 and still a investor there when it was above 11,000; a retired member of the New York Stock Exchange.

ADVICE: "Always buy the leading companies in their field, particularly technology-based companies or companies that understand technology as they will lead the market." Sonny's best picks in the technology field are Cisco, Dell, Intel, Sun MicroSystems and Amgen.

BEST INVESTMENT: "Probably Cisco CSCO Systems. Within just a few years the investment was up sevenfold." Why? Because it's the best company in its field and with the Internet Sonny believes it will continue to grow.

WORST INVESTMENT: "Redhat Inc. RHAT bought this at $65, down from $151 as a speculative venture; the price looked right but wrong. Went as low as $15; now at $19. If you're wrong on a stock, admit it and get out. Even with 30 years' experience, I just sat there and watched it go down and down and down and did nothing."

HOWARD KELLY, Entrepreneur

Former president of KD Manufacturing in Kingston, Ontario; now marketing director for Purcell Construction Corporation in Watertown, New York. One of the best sales guys I know, but it took him 25 years to realize it.

ADVICE: "Don't miss the boat. We're all in the same boat, and it wasn't raining when Noah built the ark, which translates into everyone has basically the same opportunities. Plan ahead and take advantage. Life is all about timing and making good, well-thought-out decisions. Mine have not always been as brilliant as I would have hoped, but no one will ever accuse me of sitting on the fence or not enjoying myself."

BEST INVESTMENT: "Wardair (twice). I enjoyed two trips to the Caribbean with my profits. In fact, I met Max Ward on one of the trips and he was delighted to learn that I was taking a trip on his airline with the profits from his stock!"

Worst Investment: "AC Moore. I still hold this narrowly traded craft chain stock so I may yet win, but I doubt it. This was a company that I knew a lot about and I got in shortly after their IPO. Unfortunately, the stock has not dazzled others and it is currently trading at about one-third of my purchase price. In the overall scheme of things, boats have been perhaps my worst investment."

PETER LUNDGREN, Senior Vice President, Salomon Smith Barney

Of all the people I have met in the investment industry over the years, no one has made a life work of trying to understand the markets more than Peter.

Advice: "Looking back over the last 30 years, I have found an elegantly simple answer founded on a bedrock of common sense and experience: the closer you keep your money to you, with the greatest exercise of control, the more successful you will be. I could understand this if you run your own business, but I found it more difficult to apply to the debit and equity markets. The biggest body of knowledge we have is located in our own workplace or community. We all know when companies are doing well or poorly."

Best Investment: "Always the companies I have worked for have been my best investment because it is those companies that I best understand the fundamentals about and I best know the management. Salomon Smith Barney is owned by Citibank and it will be my best investment, well positioned as the largest financial institution in the world and great management—Sandy Weill."

Citigroup Sept. 01 1998–Sept. 01 2000

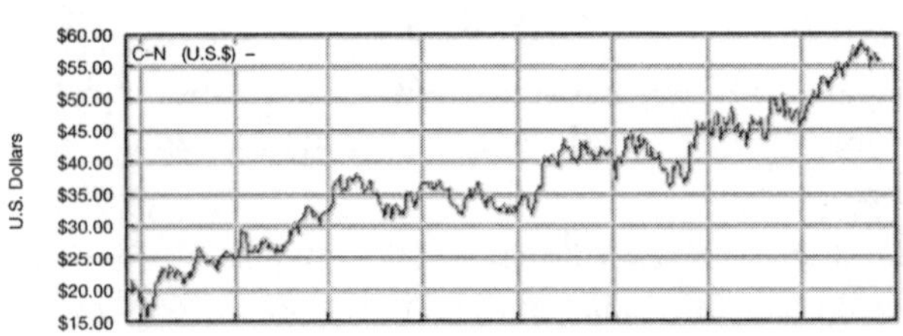

www.globeinvestor.com

WORST INVESTMENT: "The worst investment I ever made was one I understood the least about. A large finance company that specialized in lending to homeowners 125% of the equity in their homes. This was contrary to everything I understood about prudent money management. It was recommended by a well-regarded Wall Street analyst as his top pick. Unfortunately it wasn't and the stock descended from the mid-$40s to under a $1."

JOHN DRISCOLL, Chairman and CEO, NCE Resources Group
More than 30 years' experience in the oil and gas sector.

ADVICE: "Don't reinvent the wheel; success leaves tracks. Follow the management that have produced results even if they venture into a different field."

BEST INVESTMENT: "Starting and running my own company, NCE Resources."

WORST INVESTMENT: "I had to think about it, not because I haven't made any mistakes or because I have, but because I suppress them. I don't see any value in dwelling on mistakes. I like to quote the founder of GM, James Durant, who said, 'Forget past mistakes; do what you want to and do it now. Today is your lucky day.'"

BRANT SANGSTER, Vice President, Oil Sands, Petro-Canada
More than 30 years' experience in the oil industry.

ADVICE: "As a rookie, recognize that that is what you are. Set a little money aside and play with it to learn your lessons ... and maybe get some humility. Now, take the real money and put it in the hands of an expert who has the resources, data and time to make educated investment choices for you."

BEST INVESTMENT: "Petro-Canada (bought at $7.25, currently at $30.00). Petro-Canada took a beating after the IPO, but working there and knowing as much about the company as I did, I knew the value was there and it was only a matter of time until that would be recognized by the market as well."

Worst Investment: "H2O Entertainment (bought at $2.00, currently at $0.20). My son David worked for them creating video games. Instead of understanding the company from a financial point of view I got to understand it from a creative point of view and, as I found out, the two don't necessarily coincide."

NANCY TENGLER, President and CIO, Global Alliance Value Investors Ltd.

Nancy is one of the few value managers who have evolved successful methodologies, while staying true to the value style, to deal with the new economies.

Advice: "The world is changing. It's moving a lot faster and so are stock prices. Volatility studies confirm what we all see each day: stocks go up and down, at breakneck speed. In the short term price moves can blot out the single most important investment principle: investors who buy stocks are buying a piece of a company, not simply a piece of paper. Traders trade paper; investors buy companies. Investing for the long term still works, but it requires research and a healthy awareness of valuation. The correction in Internet stocks after a meteoric rise brought back perspective to the markets. Eventually fundamentals and valuation matter. Invest for the long term.

"One of the most positive changes for investors in recent years is that with the proliferation of information and opinions (and blathering for that matter) about stocks, real research is more readily available to serious-minded *investors* and that can only be good. As an individual investor, remember that discipline is the main thing. Develop your own philosophy and stick with it. At cocktail parties it is expected that you will lie about the exponential returns in your portfolio (fisherman have been doing it for years)—but stick to your discipline!"

Best Investment: "In the spring of 1999, Oracle Corporation became attractive on a valuation and fundamental basis. According to the way we look at the world, the stock had rarely been cheaper. The market was discounting slowing growth in application software. But Oracle was focused on Internet computing and the trend away from personal computers to servers. Oracle's commitment was articulated best by founder and CEO Larry Ellison who believed that the best way to demonstrate the value of the Internet to Oracle's customers was to become an Internet-centric company centered around their own products—a brilliant move that served not only to lower the company's operating expenses but also to stimulate demand for the new Internet applications. Oracle proceeded to beat estimates and 'wow' the Street. Of equal importance to us was the quality of management and the fact that Larry was 'engaged' in the company once again. Using the Larry Ellison indicator has proven to be a successful way to buy the stock—it performs better when he is in charge and not so well when he is sailing around the world in his yacht. The results? We realized around a 600% return from our acquisition price."

Oracle Sept. 01 1999–Sept. 01 2000

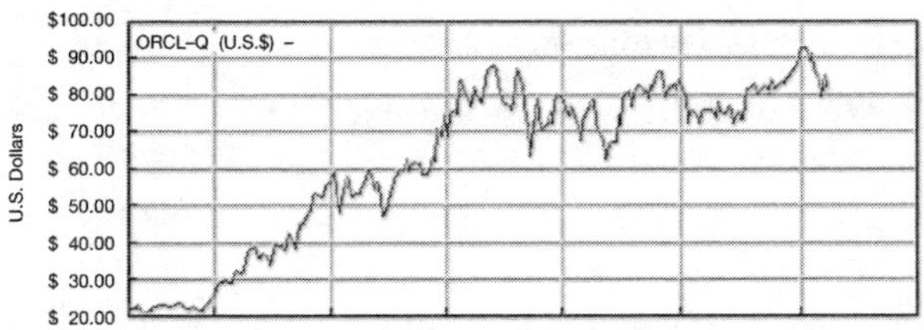

www.globeinvestor.com

WORST INVESTMENT: "Ignoring one of my long-held tenets of never taking investment tips from friends, I did something worse: I took a stock tip from a stranger of sorts. He wasn't a strange stranger; after all, I met him in first-class on a cross-country flight. He was the CFO of a company that was in the midst of an IPO road show. We didn't talk about the deal, but we did talk. After the IPO I would watch the stock from time to time. It took off and produced exponential returns for the investment bankers and early investors. After about six months the stock pulled back about 50% and I jumped in, breaking all my own rules. I knew nothing about the fundamentals of the company beyond what business they were in and I knew nothing about the management except that the CFO was a very funny guy. I bought 200 shares of Smartalk Services (SMTK) for each of my kids' college accounts. 'A little speculative growth can't hurt,' I told myself. I purchased the stock at around $16 per share after an earnings disappointment. The first warning is rarely the last. The stock was eventually de-listed and the company filed for bankruptcy. When I can get a value for my shares it shows a price of pennies per share.

"I did just about everything wrong in that transaction, but the most critical error was buying stock in a company I knew nothing about. I didn't follow my discipline and I *gambled* with my hard-earned money. Although I will never salvage the loss, the shares remain in the account as a painful reminder of my error."

JONATHAN WENER, President and CEO, Canderel Management Inc.
Never afraid to invest in new ventures if the management is good and they have fire in their belly.

Advice: "You have to invest in people. Machines depreciate; people appreciate. I would rather invest in an average product with excellent management, than a great product with an average management team. Oh yes, the management team must always have equity—a piece of the action."

Best Investment: "BCE Emergis. Bought at $6, sold at $125 in six months. I made the investment based on the people; the management team had passion, unalterable commitment and the intelligence to make it happen."

Chart BCE Emergis Sept. 01 1998–Sept. 01 2000

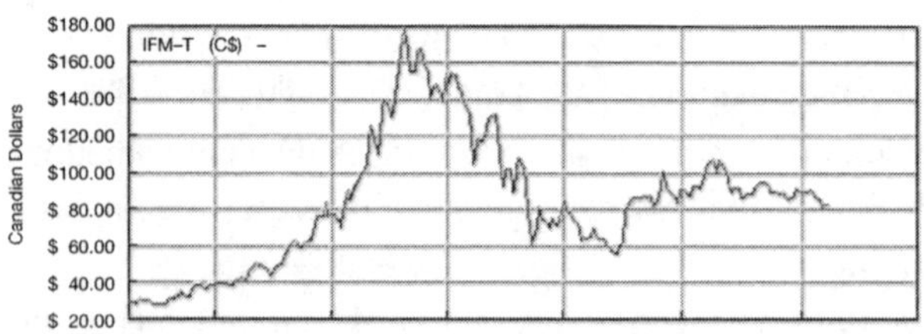

www.globeinvestor.com

Worst Investment: "Anytime I didn't follow my rule about knowing the management team, particularly a rubber recycling company called Greensback. It had poor management and went into bankruptcy, but I bought the company out of bankruptcy and turned it around with good management."

PAUL LABARGE, Senior Partner, LaBarge Weinstein

Through his own drive and initiative, Paul has positioned himself and his law firm as a key entrepreneurial component of Silicon Valley North.

Advice: "I would suggest that, in the absence of being able to conduct due diligence at a personal level and having knowledge of both the marketplace and the ability to assess directly the quality of the management team in their performance, investors should isolate investment advisers who have access to analysts' reports that are diligent and properly analyze the opportunity, the competitive pressures and the ability of the company to perform.

"Both [best and worst investments] were private companies, both represented emerging technologies and areas of business. The lesson to be drawn from both cases is substantially the same."

Best Investment: "In the case of the best investment, the return was 100 times the original investment. The crucial factors in determining the quality of an investment relate to an analysis of the competitive marketplace, the effectiveness and honesty of the management group and the ability to execute in accordance with the plan. In the best case, the management group was intelligent, motivated, focused, honest and effective in meeting milestones. As well, the company was vigilant about its financial resources and always well funded throughout its existence."

Worst Investment: "In the case of the worst investment, the entire amount of the investment was lost. The management group was dishonest and unable to execute in accordance with the plan. The constant non-performance was not redressed in the early stages and the company was insufficiently funded to be able to achieve its targets."

JONATHAN CHEVREAU, one of Canada's premier financial columnists and writers

I reminded him of his Y2K call and he reminded me that it was based on historic precedent inasmuch as the Dark Ages were a Y1K problem.

Advice: "Get either a managed-money solution or a veteran investment adviser you can trust, then stick with them for decades."
Best Investment: "Microsoft and it's not over yet."
Worst Investment: "Trying to time the market over Y2K."

"Technology will strengthen democracies in every country and at every level."
Bill Gates

ADAM CHOWANIEC, President and CEO, Tundra Semiconductor Corporation

The 1999 Ottawa Businessman of the Year. Chair of the Ottawa Economic Development Corporation. One of the key players in the creation of Silicon Valley North.

Advice: "I still believe that for the next decade investing in the companies that provide communications infrastructure to the world are the key companies to focus on—principally because they should produce good and sustainable growth as demands for more bandwidth continue to drive the need for new infrastructure."

Tundra Sept. 01 1999–Sept. 01 2000

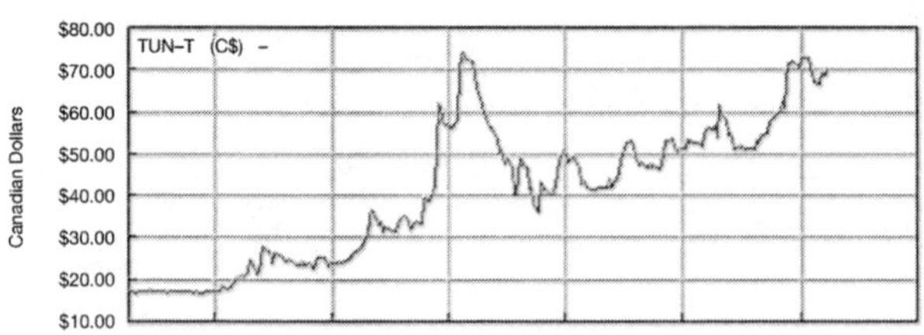

www.globeinvestor.com

BEST INVESTMENT: "If you're lucky enough to find an opportunity to build your own company. In this case our company Tundra's new issue price was $9.25 and the original private round was at $2; it now trades at greater than $70."

WORST INVESTMENT: "A bunch of little gold mines that turned out to be worth nothing. But generally the resource sector has not been kind to me. McKenzie Oil sticks in my mind; it eventually went to zero."

PAUL BATES, President, Schwab Canada

One of the true pioneers in the discount direct brokerage industry in Canada; always an innovator. Paul is a member of the board of directors of the TSE.

ADVICE: "Learn how to calculate future value and present value. By having a complete understanding of the choice of firstly whether to invest a dollar or spend a dollar, and then to understand the impact of a target rate of return over time, you will get the most from every discretionary dollar you have. You will also have a crystal-clear view of the impact of expenses, taxes and the result of reaching too far from median rates of return for given asset classes. Most people simply put off investing too long, ignore opportunities to minimize taxes and expenses, and then reach for too much risk."

BEST INVESTMENT: "My own business 'Priority and Porthmeor Securities'; I knew the industry and I picked the management team. The payoff came when we were acquired by Charles Schwab."

WORST INVESTMENT: "Live cattle future. It was pure speculation, and I didn't know enough."

DAVID CORK, broker and author of the bestseller *The Pig in the Python*

I hired him out of the government in 1984 into McLeod Young and Weir; from the start he had what it takes.

ADVICE: "After nearly 20 years in the investment business I have learned a few things along the road, sometimes the hard way. On the positive side the best advice I could give to anyone is stick to quality. I'm sure this is no great revelation to anyone, but it amazes me the number of times I have seen someone pass up a good bank stock to buy the latest craze. Stick to quality and be patient."

Best Investment: "Getting into the investment business."

Worst Investment: "On the negative side, the toughest lesson I learned was about momentum. It's not so pleasant when it works against you. When a company goes bad, even a great company, the wheels can fall off in a hurry. We have seen this lately with Laidlaw, but my biggest lesson occurred with Royal Trust, early in my career. It had been a great company for so long that it was hard to believe what was happening. My advice is that when things turn down, don't average down and don't try to pick the bottom. It is always smarter to cut your losses and look for something else."

RICHARD STONE, President and CEO, Stone & Co.

Richard is never short of determination and ingenuity; he has done it on his own.

Advice: "Do your own homework and don't invest for a small win."

Best Investment: "In the early '80s, I was a buyer of General Cinema convertible bonds, not because I cared for GC's theater chain or Pepsi distribution contracts. These convertible bonds had the option to convert into RJR common shares and at the time at a discount to RJR's stock. I had an 8% yield and the call on RJR at a discount to the market. I started buying the bonds at $83 in the mid-'80s and tendered to the KKR deal at $240. The holding period was less than three years."

Worst Investment: "Buying CT under the pretext that the controlling shareholder block could complete its share restructuring at the prices it indicated. They lost, and I lost. I put the position in before going on holidays and lost money every day I was away, while having no access to research (pre-Internet era). It's not the dollar loss that makes it the worst, it's the stress I had while on vacation and the breach of my investment process."

JOSEPH CANAVAN, President and CEO, Synergy Mutual Funds

One of Canada's fastest growing mutual fund companies. Joe always has a plan.

ADVICE: "Like anything in life, a well-designed plan is essential. Many investors will just throw money at the market with the objective of their asset pool growing. Though this can work, it will probably be erratic and will not maximize potential returns.

"It is best to build a financial plan on a foundation of debt management, only after this is accomplished should you design an investment portfolio factoring in asset allocation, geographic allocation, style allocation and possibly sector allocation.

"This process is challenging to design and execute initially, but durable and powerful longer term. It is much like building your dream home. It is best to build using a well thought out architectural blueprint and on the best possible foundation. Your home will withstand the elements, require minimal maintenance and bring you tremendous joy in the short, medium and longer term."

BEST INVESTMENT: "Early in my career I lived modestly and invested every incremental dollar in our funds. I allocated more money to the new funds, as our portfolio managers have significant advantages in managing new, smaller pools of capital with significant fund flows into them. This is one of the investing secrets most investors miss."

WORST INVESTMENT: "Buying silver during the exuberance in precious metals in the early '80s. An example of going with the herd mentality, hoping to make money on my investment but not having a well-designed plan. (I still have the silver bars.)"

MARIA HOWES, one of Canada's true fee-for-service planners

Always looks at the whole picture.

ADVICE: "Don't get into serious debt when buying a car; it's only transportation to get you from A to B. Expensive car loans are the black holes of personal finance."

BEST INVESTMENT: "Journey's End; because I sold it at a good profit."

WORST INVESTMENT: "Units in a gold trust for my RRSP—I bought them at gold's highest price from a friend who was just starting out in the brokerage business!"

KEVIN WOLF, President and COO, Bissett & Associates
One of Canada's premier growth managers and a student of the investment industry.

Advice: "Invest in yourself. If at all possible go into business for yourself or get some ownership in the company you work for. But when it comes to straight investing most people should look to managed money; don't do it yourself."

Best Investment: "The investment I made in Bissett, which was an investment in myself and a team that I believed in."

Worst Investment: "Buying on rumor even when I believe the source should know what they are talking about. I think I have learned my lesson."

JOE MCDONALD, VP, YMG Capital Management Inc.
With over 20 years' experience in Canadian mutual fund sales, Joe is one of the best salespeople in the business.

Advice: "Always do your homework; never buy companies that are over-leveraged. Buy stocks, bonds or mutual funds that fit your risk profile. Let time do the rest. If your investments are keeping you up at night, sell them."

Best Investment: "I bought solid, financially strong, well-run companies for the long term and companies that have strong brand recognition with their industry such as Trimark, Microsoft and Berkshire Hathaway."

Worst Investment: "I purchased a stock on the advice of a friend without doing my own research, and the stock went to 3 cents."

Now it's my turn to provide some pearls of wisdom. Start by building a portfolio; if you want to trade individual securities limit that activity to 25% of the whole; and do your homework before you buy any individual stock.

My best investment has clearly been putting my investments in a portfolio, starting with Sovereign and then Harmony and now Opus 2 Direct. My capital has been protected and it just keeps growing. As for individual stocks, consider the example of Virtek Vision. I knew the stock very well, and I was on the board and responsible for finding the new president. I accumulated the stock over a four-year period, always with a target price in mind, and sold when it hit the target price—near-perfect execution. Time will tell if I sold too soon.

Perfect execution does not mean buying at the bottom and selling at the top; only people at cocktail parties do that. It means doing the research, choosing the right stock, accumulating it within your preset buying range, watching it carefully, preserving capital and selling it when it hits your preset target. Buying at the bottom and selling at the top is not a plan, it's fantasy. Don't worry about selling too soon; all the great investors do.

In terms of my worst investment, like most other investors, I have a few to choose from. For me, it had to be the Domino's Pizza Parlour in Cornwall, Ontario. Suffice it to say that I knew nothing about pizzas and even less about Cornwall. Management wasn't up to the task, and three new competitors moved in just before a major plant closed. Bad management, too much competition and dwindling client base—what more could you ask for? The best thing I can say about the whole experience was it was quick so no one suffered long.

There is no doubt that the considerable experiences of these investors reveal some interesting trends, but three stand out. First, **tax-driven** investments haven't generally done well; second, without **good management** nothing goes right; and third, involving yourself with something you know nothing about or failing to **do your research** inevitably leads to disaster.

Tax Shelters

Jim Muir seems to be the only one of our group who has turned a tax-driven investment into his best investment; generally, it seems that if it's tax driven it's not likely to be investment quality and if it's investment quality it doesn't need to be tax driven. Our investors seem not to have had much luck with tax-driven investments, and many of them complained about the illiquid nature of these investments and changing tax rulings that added considerably to their problems. Years ago, a client when approached about a tax deal told me, "I hate paying taxes, but I would rather lose 50 cents on the dollar to taxes than 100 cents on the dollar to a bad investment." That's advice worth noting.

Tom Kierans admits to making his best investment by ignoring tax advice and John Smith points out that tax issues are not a consideration when he looks for an investment, so be warned, and I have more than once reduced my profits by trying to time capital gains. So when it comes to tax considerations our investors' experiences show that they are not conducive to enhancing profits.

> "The hardest thing in the world to understand is the income tax."
>
> *Albert Einstein*

Management

Management—what can you say about management? I once had the pleasure of meeting Big Ben and Ian Millar, Canada's most successful equestrian partnership. We began talking about great riders and great horses and about the partnership between horse and rider—after all, who would know more about great riders and great horses than Ian Millar and Big Ben? So I ask, "If I got on Big Ben, how well could I do?" I am sure Ian was thinking about the difference between getting on and staying on, but at least he was polite enough not to laugh. "A great horse can take a mediocre rider to a good finish," he responds. Never content to leave well enough alone, I ask, "But can a great rider take a bad horse far?" "Absolutely not," is his response. So it is with management: no matter how good the idea, without great management nothing profitable will happen. In fact, if you ask around within the ranks of venture capitalists they will tell you that there is no shortage of good ideas in Canada today, but there is a real shortage of skilled managers to execute these opportunities.

Sometimes you can get an industry that is so strong that it will allow poor management to do well, but it is likely to be a short-lived phenomenon. I am not saying that great management teams can take a bad business plan and make money, but a great idea without good management will surely lose money, and the corollary is that if you combine a great idea with a great management team you can hit a home run.

Carefully check out the management team; many of our investors have run into trouble because their investments were not driven by good management teams and many of our investors have profited from the actions of great managers such as Fairfax Financial's Prem Watsa, Citigroup's Sandy Weill and BCE Emergis's Brian Edwards. Investor Jonathan Wener believes that it always comes down to management: "Companies with great managers that have fire in their bellies and a piece of the action, that's where you will find success." In several situations, the investors themselves have been instruments in replacing or placing good management in companies they invest in to ensure a profitable outcome.

For a surprising number of our pundits, good management meant starting their own company and handpicking their own management teams. For them, it appeared to be the fastest route to good management. This is a surefire way to ensure that senior management thinks the way you do.

Research

There seems to be no alternative (not even luck) to being well informed when it comes to investing, particularly if one is selecting individual securities.

"Diligence is the mother of good luck."
Benjamin Franklin

For almost all of our investors, their best investments were in areas they knew a lot about or had carefully researched. And almost all of their biggest losses came when they ventured outside of their areas of expertise or failed to do proper level of research. Clearly this principle will also apply to you. What is surprising is that almost everyone of us knew at the time that what we were doing was a low-probability investment exercise and that we were breaking the investment rules we had set for ourselves. Whether it is greed or hubris, it's not investing—it's gambling. However, each of these investors was wise enough to restrict the amount of capital risked to a very small percentage of the whole. So, while they will readily admit that an uninformed investment in an area you know nothing about is most certainly a foolish act, none were foolish enough to allow this type of investment to affect their investment capital in a serious way.

Which leads me to one of my most interesting observations: people who have serious money are concerned primarily about risk to capital; yes they also want performance, but not if it represents any serious risk to capital. Those with smaller amounts of money seem to be fixated on not just performance but short-term performance; again if you want to be wealthy you have to do what wealthy people do.

"I find that the harder I work, the more luck I seem to have."
Thomas Jefferson

There appears to be no shortcut, if not for Thomas Jefferson and Benjamin Franklin, then certainly not for you or me. Stay within areas that you understand or research new areas carefully before you venture beyond the familiar. If you feel unsure, stay within the bounds of a properly designed investment portfolio and do not take on the risk of individual stock purchases.

My father always told the story of a man that goes to an old country doctor for advice because when he raises his arm high above his head it hurts, whereupon the doctor advises him to stop raising his arm so high above his head. If you attempt to enhance your investment performance by the purchase of individual securities and time and again it does not yield a positive result, stop purchasing individual securities and let the professionals do the investing for you through a properly designed portfolio of funds.

If you are just beginning to invest, save your money and concentrate on portfolio construction. If you are an experienced investor, make the appropriate alterations to your portfolio. If you choose to trade individual stocks, restructure your personal investment process today, and make sure that 75% of your assets are in your properly designed portfolio so that when the Dow hits 40,000 and the TSE hits 20,933 on or about January 1, 2007, you'll be there and you'll receive your fair share.

What really matters at the end of the day is being in the market. You can't create wealth as a spectator of the financial markets. The real risk is being out of the markets, not in the markets. You cannot create wealth by watching from the sidelines.

"Ideas are easy. It's execution that's hard."
Jeff Bezos (Amazon.com)

Index